BETWEEN PRISON AND PALACE

Carmelyon

BETWEEN PRISON AND PALACE

THE PARISH OF ST GEORGE SOUTHWARK BEFORE THE REFORMATION

TONY LUCAS

Carmelyon

First published in 2004
Revised edition 2009

ISBN 978-0-9561521-1-4

Published by Carmelyon
23 Clements Road,
London SE16 4DW

CONTENTS

ILLUSTRATIONS

PREFACE

Martha Carlin, in her book on M*edieval Southwark,* writes of St George's that "its medieval records have not survived and its history is largely unknown." How some of those records came to be lost is related by an earlier historian of the parish, William Rendle. He tells us that, "We might have had a more complete record of the old church, but unfortunately, in 1776, the parish papers and documents were sold in a lump, at the rate of 1½d the lb., the purchaser to cart them away."

The scrap dealer's cart may have been filled with Churchwardens' accounts, Guild or Vestry minutes, copies of wills and deeds, rent rolls – we shall never know. All that remains to us are the fragments of evidence which chanced to survive elsewhere, as part of other records in other places.

What I have aimed to do here is to bring together the surviving information, both to make it more easily accessible, and to look at it carefully, to see just how much it is able to tell us. It is rather like trying to assemble a jig-saw, when all but a handful of the pieces have been thrown away.

Some of the earliest people to write about St George's were the antiquarians of the 17th and 18th century – Aubrey, Hatton and the anonymous author of a hand-written description of the second church, surviving in the British Library. Much of the known information was gathered together in the monumental work of Manning & Bray on *The History and Antiquities of the County of Surrey,* 1814.

The most engaging of the later, more anecdotal, writers was William Rendle. His *Old Southwark and its People* was published in 1878 and contains many pages about St George's. Rendle knew and loved the area well, having held the office of Medical Officer of Health for St George's Parish. Over the years, other pamphlets and articles about the parish have also appeared, many of them re-cycling much the same material.

In the 20th century, the volume of The Survey of London, covering *St George's Fields* contained detailed descriptions of the fabric of the building, as well as other historical notes. In the parish itself, John Pinder did much research in the mid 20th century, and wrote a new Guide & History. Of more recent works, Martha Carlin's *Medieval Southwark* is indispensable, especially for the context of the settlement as a whole.

Extensive redevelopment of the surrounding area has meant that reports from archaeological sites have mapped out many early features of Southwark in new detail. More particularly, since the first edition of this book appeared, the underpinning of the church occasioned archaeological investigation of the site of St George's itself. Study of that material will continue for some time, but a few of the provisional findings have been incorporated in this revision.

The Southwark Local Studies Library is an excellent resource for anyone studying any aspect of Southwark and its past. I am most grateful to its patient and helpful staff and, above all, to Stephen Humphrey, the Head Librarian, whose knowledge of the field is extensive and who has always been ready to respond to my questions and to point me in directions I might not otherwise have gone. I have benefited from the resources of the British Library, the Guildhall Library, the Public Record Office, the Institute of Historical Research and, particularly, the Warburg Institute. I have also appreciated the facilities and been helped by the staff of the Record Office at Winchester – where the Registers of the medieval bishops are kept. Finally, my thanks to the people at St George's, who have a lively interest in their own history, and who were supportive of my pursuit of its detail.

Tony Lucas

ABBREVIATIONS

B.L. British Library

B.R.U.O. "A Biographical Register of the University of Oxford to AD 1500," A.B.Emden. Oxford 1957/9.

Cal. Letters Spain "Calendar of Letters and Despatches and State Papers relating to the negotiations between England and Spain, preserved in the Archives at Simancas and Elsewhere." Ed. G.A. Bergenwith. Vol. Henry VII 1485-1509.

Cal. Patent Rolls "Calendar of the Patent Rolls preserved in the Public Record Office for the reign of Henry VII." Rolls Series 1914

Cal. Papal Reg. "Calendar of Entries in the Papal registers relating to Great Britain and Northern Ireland." Ed. Michael J. Haren. Irish Manuscripts Commission 1989.

Cal. Papers Venice "Calendar of State Papers and Manuscripts relating to English Affairs existing in the Archive and Collections of Venice and in other Libraries of North Italy." Ed. Rawdon Brown 1864. Vols. 1 – 3.

M. Carlin "Medieval Southwark" by Martha Carlin, The Hambledon Press 1996

D.N.B. Dictionary of National Biography

Letters & Papers Henry VIII "Letters and Papers Foreign and Domestic of the Reign of Henry VIII preserved in the Public Record Office or elsewhere in England." Arranged and Catalogued by J.S. Brewer 1862. Second Edition revised and greatly enlarged by R.H. Brodie 1920.

Materials Henry VII. "Materials for a History of the reign of Henry VII from original documents in the Public Record Office." Ed. Revd. William Campbell. 2 Volumes. Rolls Series 1873.

P.R.O. Public Record Office.

Reg. Wayneflete (etc.) Register of Bishop Wayneflete (etc.) The Registers cited are mostly of medieval bishops of Winchester. The early ones have been edited and published, the later ones exist only in manuscript. Originals are in the County Record Office at Winchester.

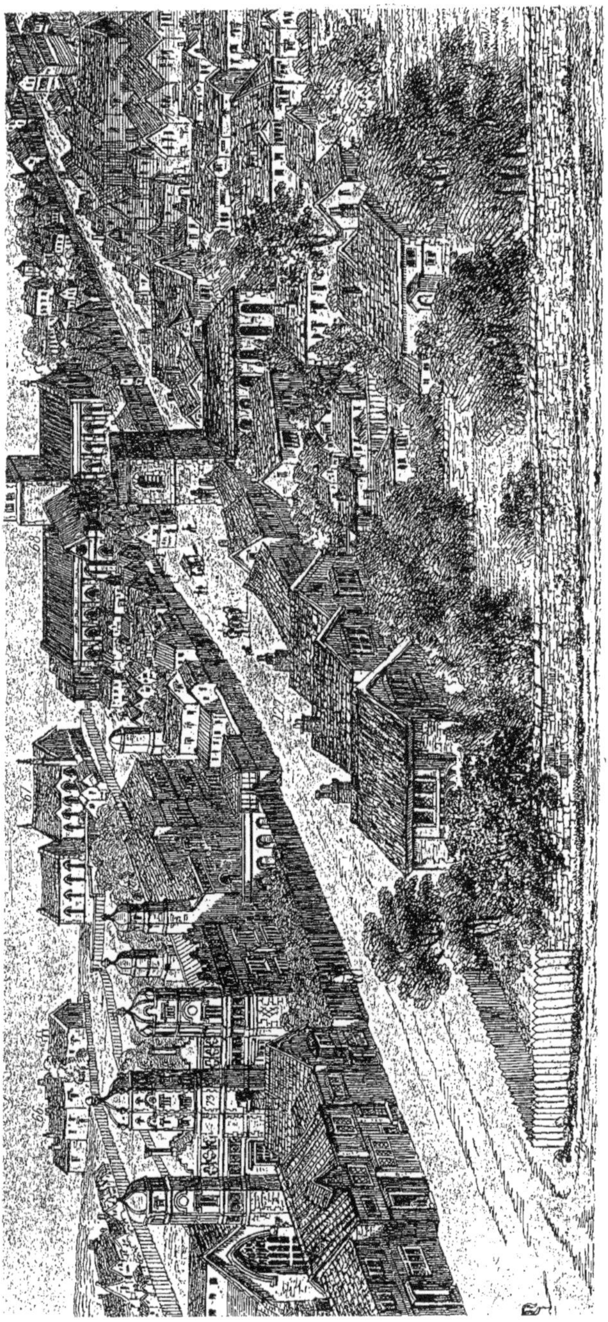

Overleaf: A 19th century drawing based on the panorama by Antonis van den Wyngaerde, showing the second church with the Brandon's palace opposite. When Wyngaerde made his original drawing in the 1540s, the church building was about halfway through its life.
(from an original in Southwark Local Studies Library)

THE BEGINNINGS OF SAINT GEORGE'S:
THOMAS ARDERN AND MONKS OF BERMONDSEY

The written history of the church of St George in Southwark begins with an entry in the Annals of Bermondsey Abbey for the year 1122. This records that the church was given to the monks, along with various tithes, by a man called Thomas of Ardern and his son Thomas. As this short text is the only evidence we have on the origins of the church, it is worth submitting it to some scrutiny, to see what it can and cannot tell us.

BEFORE 1122

The site of St George's must have had a certain significance, even before any church was built. It stands at an ancient road junction. Long before the A2 and A3, the Roman roads from Dover and from the Solent, known to us as Watling Street and Stane Street, met somewhere nearby. Indeed, there may well have been older trackways before them, leading to the river crossing.

A good deal of evidence about Roman Southwark has been uncovered by rescue archaeologists in recent years, especially since the current regeneration of the area got under way in the mid 1990s. It is being revealed as a much more extensive settlement than had previously been thought. There is now a suggestion that the boundary of the settlement lay beyond the church site. Fragments of Samian ware came out of a bore-hole in the churchyard, sunk in 1997.

Traces of a main Roman Road have been found close by, and it is conjectured that the street may have crossed the east side of the church site. The large site to the east, between Long Lane and Tabard Street, yielded evidence of clay and timber buildings and what appears to be a religious complex, with two small Romano-Celtic temples. On the church site itself evidence of clay and timber buildings was found, dating from the 1st century, a clay oven, an animal pen and various dumps. These have been provisionally interpreted as ‘ribbon’ developments along the west side of the road – probably shops or houses with yards at the back. (1)

There seems to be little or no evidence of occupation during the next few centuries after Roman rule ended. There is no recorded mention of Southwark until the early 900s. Two churches are mentioned in the Domesday Book of 1086, but the Domesday account of `Sudwerca’ is not easy to relate to the settlement as it developed. The listing is by landholders and may not even cover the land around St George’s. Where mention is made of a church, it is not identified. St Mary’s (now the Cathedral) and St Olave’s (which was east of the Bridge) are considered the likely candidates. This may not totally rule out the possible existence of the church before 1086, but it certainly offers no positive evidence for it.

PARISH BOUNDARIES

It has been pointed out that the rather strange boundaries of the ancient parish of St George may themselves be a clue to where it fits in the Southwark sequence. (2) The awkward L-shape of the parish seems to be a consequence of its being wrapped around the northern boundaries of Newington Manor. Until a very recent boundary change, people on the south side of Great Dover Street, who looked out of their windows directly at St George’s church, were not within its official parish.

This may well imply that Newington Manor was already in existence when the parish was formed, and that St George’s was fitted into a gap that remained between Newington and the various riverside properties, taking up areas that were not clearly assigned to any other parish before that time.

CRUSADERS

The other possible clue may be in the name of the church. It is said to be the earliest documented dedication to St George in London. The cult of St George is a complex study in itself. There is scarcely any firm historical evidence about the saint. If there was a real person behind the stories, then he was a soldier, martyred during the persecution under the reign of the Emperor Diocletian, and perhaps at Lydda in Palestine. The date would have been close to 300 AD. His cult spread widely in the east.

The earliest sure evidence for St George being known in Britain is his inclusion in a calendar of saints, drawn up by Bede in the early 8th century. However, it was only with the Crusaders that his popularity in the West took root. The first Crusade was during the years 1097-99. St George is said to have appeared in a vision at Antioch, at a turning point in the campaign. Perhaps the best guess we can make about the origins of the church is that it might have been built soon after 1100, and may have had a connection with someone returning – or failing to return – from the Crusade. (3)

Anyone going from England on that expedition would be most likely to have joined the army led by Robert, Duke of Normandy, eldest son of William the Conqueror, together with his brother-in-law Stephen, Count of Blois. They set out from northern France in October 1096 and made their way to Italy. There they wintered in Calabria and did not cross the sea until the following April. They marched across the Balkans, spent two weeks at Constantinople, then crossed into Asia, to join the main army at the siege of Nicea. Duke Robert started his return journey home quite soon after the capture of Jerusalem in the summer of 1099.

It would all be much simpler if we could link the name of Ardern to that campaign, or any other major events of the period. But records are much more sparse for this period than they were even a century later, and the evidence does not exist. We need to look carefully at the one record we do have, and see just how much it might be able to suggest.

THE DONATION

The first question to be asked, is how reliable is the evidence of the Bermondsey Annals? One might expect that monastic chroniclers would be trustworthy, but when it came to recording their property rights – especially if they were being contested – it is by no means unknown for evidence to be 'improved', when deeds and charters were being copied.

The Annals of Bermondsey are relatively short, and were written quite late. They survive in a single manuscript, now in the British Library, seventy-one of whose vellum pages have been inscribed. (4) They are written in the same hand throughout, in a clear Gothic cursive script, which is dated to the mid 15th century. The presentation gives the impression of its having been written by someone who had ample time for the task in hand. The manuscript appears to have been consulted very little, and it has almost the freshness of a modern facsimile edition, rather than a medieval original.

This does mean that, unlike some more famous Chronicles, they are of little value as a record of wider historical events. Their main interest now is confined to the history of the Abbey itself. The annals cover the years from 1042 to 1432. The date 1433 has been added, but with no entry, which suggests that this may be the likely date of composition. Although a gap of 300 years between an event and its recording would seriously reduce the value of the evidence for, say, a political event, for the record of a property donation, such as we are considering, it could be argued that it strengthens the reliability. After that gap of time, it is unlikely that anyone would be contesting the Abbey's ownership of St George's, and so there may have been no incentive for any tampering with whatever record the scribe used to copy his account.

The text of the entry reads as follows:

Anno Domini MCXXII et anno regni Henrici primi vicesimo secundo. Hoc anno Thomas de Ardern et Thomas filius ejus dederunt monachis de Bermundeseye ecclesiam Sancti Georgii in Southwerk, et decimas de dominio suo in blado in Horndone, et terram de ponte Londiniae quinque solidos per annum reddentem; et totam minutam decimam in praedicta villa, ut in lanis, caseis, in agnis, in vitulis, in pullis equinis, et in omnibus aliis rebus decimandis. Quam concessionem de ecclesia Sancti Georgii concessit et confirmavit Henricus primus.

'The year of our Lord 1122 and the twenty-second year of the reign of Henry I. In this year Thomas of Ardern and Thomas his son gave to the monks of Bermondsey the church of Saint George in Southwark, and tithes of his estate in corn in Horndon, and land of London bridge returning five *solidos* a year; and the whole lesser tithe in the aforesaid settlement, as in wool, in cheese, in lambs, in calves, in young horses, and in all other things titheable. Which grant of the church of Saint George was granted and confirmed by Henry I.'

WHO WERE THE ARDERNS?

There is little evidence about this family before 1122, but there is a certain amount to be discovered from then onwards. The estate in Horndon was not some ancestral seat, but holdings which they seem to have acquired in that same year.

Horndon-on-the-Hill lies just north-west of Standford le Hope. It remains an attractive small village, with a number of early buildings, its hilltop position looking out across the A13 toward the Thames estuary. In the Domesday Book it is referred to as 'Horniduna', and two manors are listed: one held by Count Eustace of Boulogne, the other by 'Edmund son of Algot'. It is this latter property which is thought to have passed into the possession of the Ardern family, and it came to be known as Ardern Hall.

The Domesday Book describes it as *"held by 2 free men as manor and as 2½ hides and 15 acres in King Edward's time. Then 3 ploughs on the desmesne; now 2. Then 2 ploughs belonging to the men; now 1. Then as now 1 villein. Then 14 bordars; now 16. Then 3 serfs; now none. Pasture for 50 sheep, 12 acres of meadow. Then 5 beasts, 1 rouncey, 20 swine, 150 sheep; now 35 sheep. It is worth 50 shillings. There is also a certain deacon who has 30 acres and a fourth part of the church; and it is in the king's gift."*

The family held a number of other lands in Essex, during the years that followed. Matching Hall, which lies more than 20 miles north, to the east of Harlow, had passed, by 1216, to a Thomas de Arderne, who is identified as being of the same family. (5) They held it for much of that century, and seem to have made themselves unpopular in the locality by closing off much of the open woodland into a park. In the second half of the 13th century, Housham Hall in Matching was held by a Ralph de Arderne, and he and his wife had an interest in Quickbury Manor, nearby in Sheering, which had also been the subject of a grant to Bermondsey Abbey. (6)

Arderns continue to appear in the records of Essex, as landed gentry, throughout the medieval period.

Several different accounts are given of the possible origin of the name 'Arden', but it is almost certainly related to the word, of Celtic origin, which linked 'woods' with a 'high place' and gave rise to both the Forest of Arden in Warwickshire and the Ardennes in Belgium. There was a Warwickshire family of the same name, said to be "one of the very few English families that can trace their ancestry back to before the Norman Conquest." (7) They trace their descent from an Anglo-Saxon nobleman called Aelfwine, who was sheriff of Warwick in the mid 11th century. His son, Thurkill of Warwick, also known as Thurkill de Ardern, so ingratiated himself with the Norman conquerors that he held more lands, as the Domesday Book shows, than any other non-Norman Englishman.

Probably no evidence exists to connect the Arderns in Warwickshire with those in Essex, though they seem to have been of similar status, as gentry whose names occur in records of property transactions and grants to churches throughout the middle ages. It is an interesting coincidence, however, that 'Edmund, son of Algot' who held the manor of Horndon at the time of Domesday, was also an Englishman. (8) Although nothing can be proved, it does invite speculation that the family might have been of partly Anglo-Saxon origin. Having managed to hold a place for themselves under the new Norman establishment, what we may now glimpse in the grant of St George's is, perhaps, a step in the process of securing their place.

Certainly, a gift to Bermondsey Priory would have been a favourite way of doing this. The house had been founded forty years earlier, during the reign of William the Conqueror, and was linked to the great abbey of Cluny, which had been in the forefront of monastic reform during that century. It was founded by a London citizen, called Alwin Child, and soon afterward the king granted the manor of Bermondsey to the Priory. The house continued to receive patronage from the Norman kings, even from William Rufus, who was not noted for his generosity toward the church. This royal patronage also helped Bermondsey to attract many other benefactions, because giving to the Priory could be seen as a way of showing both loyalty to the Crown and generosity toward the Church at the same time.

It is possible that the donation of St George's, with accompanying tithes, by the Arderns could have been a way of oiling the wheels of a process by which they received royal approval of their new acquisition of property at Horndon, and confirmation of their rights.

CHURCH BUILDING AND PATRONAGE

We might also want to ask how a family like this would come to own rights in a parish church, and why they should be giving these to a local monastery? In fact, what we see happening here fits well into the context of its time.

From about the middle of the tenth century, there seems to have been a steady increase in population over much of Western Europe, with the clearing of unused land and creation of new settlements and estates. Many estates appear to have been provided with local churches, at this time, which they may never have had before. The French historian Rodolfus Glaber, himself a monk of Cluny, wrote in the mid eleventh century of a new abundance and stability, and of the land being 'white with churches' that were being newly built.

Many of these parish churches would have been built by the lord of the manor for his family and tenants, and he and his heirs would have appointed the priests who served their church. However, during the second half of the eleventh century, a strong movement of reform began to influence church appointments. Often reform movements start on the margins of society and move inward, but this one began at the centre, in Rome itself. A group of people gathered together by Pope Leo IX (1049-54), which included the theologian Peter Damian and the deacon Hildebrand, later to become Pope Gregory VII (1073-85), shared concerns about simony, about marriage of the clergy, and also about lay control over church appointments.

Gregory VII engaged in a famous power struggle with the German Emperor Henry IV, and later, Anselm, archbishop of Canterbury, was involved in a series of disputes with the English kings William II and Henry I. But the campaign against `lay investiture' reached beyond issues about the appointment of bishops and popes, and created a climate that was hostile to the appointment of clergy by laymen at the local level as well. A Church Council at Clermont in 1095, for instance, ruled that "No altars or tithes and above all no churches may remain in lay hands. Those who own them are to be warned and implored to give them up. If they do not do so after repeated warnings they are to be excommunicated." (9) In fact there was never any systematic campaign against local lay patronage - nothing as intense as the battle waged against lay investiture of bishops - and many parish churches did remain in lay hands. Nevertheless, a climate was created which led to many others being transferred at this time, especially as gifts to monastic houses.

In principle, there is no reason why the ownership of tithes and rights of patronage by a monastery should be any better than ownership by a lay magnate. However, the reformers of this period placed a high value on the monastic life, as well as exalting the clergy in general above the laity. Ownership by monasteries was never brought into question. There was a considerable element of double thinking here. Not only had so many of the new churches been founded by lay people, but also the monastic orders and the reform movement itself relied heavily on the laity for financial support, for recruitment of personnel, and sometimes for military backing in situations of conflict.

One writer on this period says that "religious houses in the period from the late eleventh to the early thirteenth century acquired parish churches on a scale not equalled before or since." (10) The exact extent of this transfer has proved hard to quantify, but it has been suggested that before 1200 a quarter of the parish churches of England were in the hands of religious communities. (11)

TITHES

The real value to the monastery of such transactions, was in the payment of tithes that went with them. The idea of giving a tenth of the produce of the land for the support of public worship and the priesthood, goes back to the Old Testament, and passed into the early church. From the Carolingian period it began to be established in legislation. There were many local and regional variations but, in general, it could be seen as something like a `value added tax' set at 10%.

Often a distinction was made between the 'greater' tithe, raised on the main cereal crops, and a 'lesser' tithe raised on livestock, vegetables and other smaller items. This can clearly be seen in the text about St George's, which specifies the main tithe on both properties and adds the lesser tithe from Horndon, listing some of the main categories on which it was to be levied – wool, cheese, lambs, calves, etc. The twelfth century was a period of high inflation in England and, another writer says, "Wise abbots everywhere naturally sought to acquire and recover tithes as a protection against rising prices, which reduced the real value of their revenues in money."(12) Tithes offered to the monastery a form of income that was 'index-linked', rising with inflation.

Tithes were attached to the property, rather than to the individual, as our text again shows. One portion of the tithe – usually a quarter or a third – was intended for the maintenance of the parish priest. Other portions were supposed to go to the upkeep of the fabric of the church, for relieving the needs of the poor, and to the bishop. Sometimes these payments would have been appropriated by unscrupulous landlords. But what happened when they passed into the hands of a monastery?

Clearly the tithes from Horndon would not have been helping to support the local parish church there. In theory, it might appear that they were being assigned to help provide for the upkeep of St George's, which may not have had much endowment of its own, as a recently founded urban church. In practice though, the tithes would have gone toward the general income of Bermondsey Priory, and any provision for St George's probably came out of that.

There was some dispute, between bishops and abbots, about the diversion of tithes to monasteries, and one or two papal decrees of the late eleventh century tried to set some limits on the practice. (13) A Council at Westminster in 1102 said that monks should not 'despoil' the parishes they owned to an extent that made the situation of the priests difficult or prevented the proper service of the altar. (14) Nevertheless, the transfer of assets continued. By this period, most monks were ordained and so they were regarded as being entitled to offerings for the clergy; also, because of their vow of poverty, they claimed a right to those tithes set aside for the poor.

SUMMARY

The short entry in the Bermondsey Annals for 1122 is like a small window opened on the obscurity of the early history of the parish. What it seems to show us is a transaction which accords well with its historical context. The dedication of the church fits within its period, and suggests something about the concerns of the founder. We see the lay owners moving with the spirit of the times, and transferring the patronage to a monastery, but probably doing so at a time and in a manner that helped secure their own status as land-owners, by gaining royal approval.

Thomas Ardern and his son would have gained merit through their gift to the church, as well as the spiritual benefits of a link with a major house of prayer. As benefactors of the Priory, they could expect to continue to be remembered in prayer by the monks. At the same time, they were seen to be supporting a foundation which was favoured by the royal family, and they received king Henry's approval for the whole transaction, which included their other property. If, by any chance, they were a family with Anglo-Saxon origins, this would have been especially important for them, in helping secure their place within a society dominated by the Normans.

NOTES

1. See *'St George's Church....An archaeological post-excavation assessment'* J. Taylor & B. Watson, Museum of London Archaeology Service 2007.
2. The former church of St George, Botolph Lane, in the City of London is known to have existed in the reign of Henry II. There may be a parallel with churches named for St George in those that had a dedication of the 'Holy Sepulchre'. These also begin in England in the 12th Century, and are likely to have originated with visits to Jerusalem.
3. MS Harleian 231. British Library. Transcribed in Luard, *Annales Monastici iii.*
4. *Rotula Litterarum Clausarum* Vol I, p.247
5. *Annals of Bermondsey,* ed. Luard, iii. 429.
6. *A Dictionary of Surnames,* P. Hanks & F. Hodges, Oxford 1988.
7. There were also a number of properties in Essex held under the name of 'Thurkill'.
8. Quoted from G. Tellenbach, *The church in western Europe from the tenth to the early twelfth century.* CUP 1993 p.289.
9. B.R. Kemp, "Monastic Possession of Parish Churches in England in the Twelfth Century", *Journal of Ecclesiastical History, Vol. 31, No. 2, April 1980.* p.133ff.
10. e.g. M. Brett, *The English Church under Henry I,* p.220, and Dom David Knowles, *The Monastic Order in England,* pp. 595-7.
11. Giles Constable, *Monastic Tithes from their Origins to the Twelfth Century,* Cambridge 1964, p.107.
12. Gregory VII issued decrees from a synod at Rome in 1078 which affirmed episcopal jurisdiction over the holding of tithes by abbots, and issued similar confirmations from a Synod at Melfi in 1089. These may, however, have affirmed principle rather than changed practice.
13. C.J. von Hefele, *Histoire des Conciles*, ed. & trans. by H. Leclerq, pp. 476-7

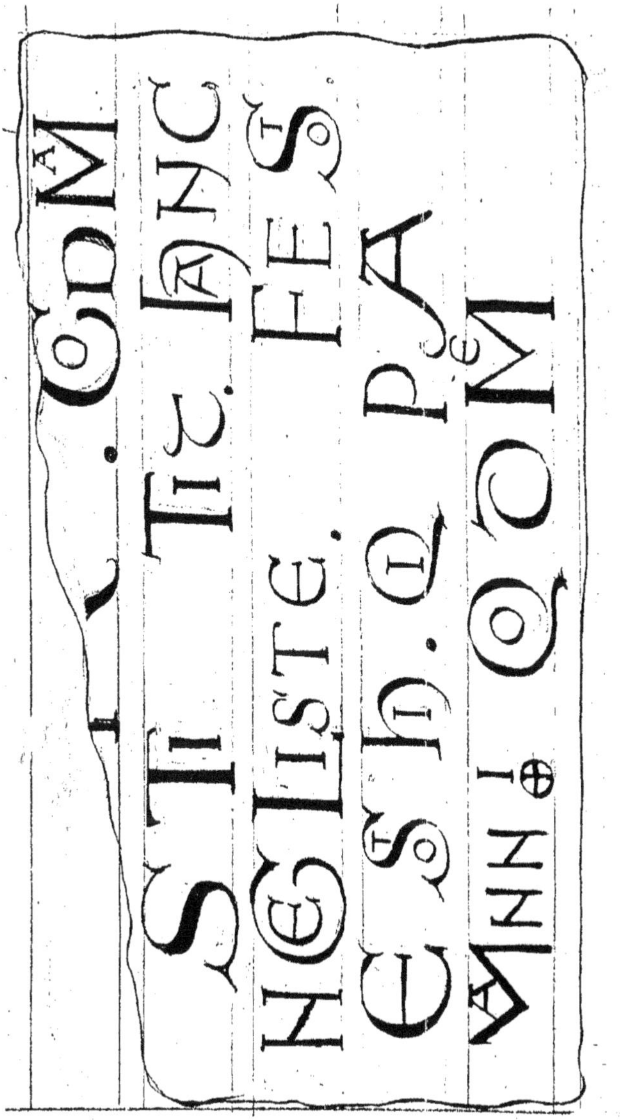

Overleaf: Transcription of the lettering on the inscribed stone found during the demolition of the church in 1733. This is the version produced for the Society of Antiquaries in 1737. (Other transcriptions do not show a letter 'I' inside the 'H' in line 4.)

A LOST STONE

I am particularly indebted to Stephen Humphrey for drawing my attention to the evidence about an inscribed stone, once part of the fabric of St George's Church, but now lost. It seems that the stone was discovered when the tower of the second church was taken down in 1733. Two early accounts of it survive,

The first is in a collection of papers, now in the British Library (MS 6402) 'bequeathed by the Revd. William Cole in 1783'. Here we find a copy of the lettering on the stone, followed by this brief description:

> ***Found on a Stone in the Middle of the Wall of the Tower of the Steeple of St George Church, Southwark. There was a Stone plac'd before this as if to preserve it.***
>
> ***The lines about 2 In distance from each other.***

Height of the Stone	***11¾ In***
Breadth	***9***
Thickness	***3***

The other brief account of the stone is to be found in an article in ***Archaeologia Vol II***, p187 ff., based on a paper read at the Society of Antiquaries by Mr Gough, on 22nd February 1770. The subject of the paper is **"*Conjectures on an antient Tomb in Salisbury Cathedral*"**, but Mr Gough compares the lettering on this tomb with three other examples –

a) an inscription on a leaden plate found in Lincoln minster,

b) the epitaph of Ilbertus in the ruins of Monkton Farleigh priory,

c) "The third is an inscription of uncertain date, found in taking down the steeple of St George's church, Southwark, 1733, communicated to this Society by Mr Ames, 1737, and here engraved from their minutes."

Figure 3 of the accompanying plate has a drawing of the stone. The detail of the lettering agrees quite closely with the version in Cole's papers. The two sketches do, however, give a rather different impression of the stone itself. Cole draws a tidy square around the letters, with just a small piece out of the top left hand corner – as if it were a slab with a small piece missing. The drawing in ***Archaeologia*** is more three-dimensional, and makes it look much more of a broken fragment.

This is surely correct. The stone, we have been told, was three inches thick. The inscription seems to be incomplete.

Underneath Cole's drawing of the stone, these words have been added in pencil:

> ***as Read by Mr Lyd***
> ***R. Codam Stitit hanc Nec esto hic qui***
> ***patietur (?) Liste quodem Festo Manni***
> ***R. Codam Raised this Be not thou he that will suffer***
> ***it to be defaced at any feast of Mannus.***

This is the first attempt at decoding what is on the stone. The 19th century writer William Rendle, commenting on this (and wrongly ascribing it to Gough), says that it "looks like an attempt to explain the unexplainable." Neither Mr Lyd's transcription nor his attempted translation makes much sense, and neither has been endorsed by anyone looking at the evidence since.

Rendle is one of the few later historians to say anything about the stone. His book on ***Old Southwark and its People***, published in 1878, gives 20 lines to the subject.. He says,"It appears to have been a quasi-Roman inscription of the eleventh and twelfth centuries, and seems to imply, says one, that an Alderman of London laid the first stone: another hints that it was probably an old Roman stone with an inscription, used in building the first church. There were many Roman villas up and down the High Street, near to the site of St George's Church...." He then gives the attempted translation above, before concluding "...Suffice it to say, it appears to be good evidence of the great antiquity of our church, and was probably taken from the remains of a Roman villa near at hand."

Whether or not the stone itself came from a Roman site – and it is not impossible that there were Roman materials still locally available to builders in the Norman period – it seems likely that Gough was correct, in comparing the lettering with other medieval examples, and placing it around the 12th century.

This means that the inscription would belong to a similar period to that in which the original church was built, and would therefore increase the likelihood that this may have been a stone preserved from the original building – part of a memorial or, maybe, even a foundation stone. The fact that it was placed in the tower, with another stone set in front – as Cole says, "as if to preserve it" – might be taken to strengthen that hypothesis.

As to the inscription itself, we can at least avoid the kind of improbable reading given in Cole's notes, if we recognise that the stone is almost certainly broken and missing part of its text on the left hand side. The reason for asserting this is partly the broken ***M (?)*** at the beginning of the last line, but more particularly the first word in line 3. It has been proposed, very plausibly, that this should read ***(EVA)NGELISTE FESTO*** – 'the feast of the evangelist....' If such a reading were correct, it would fit well with this being some sort of commemorative tablet – recording the date of a death, or of a dedication.

Of the four Evangelists, the one most often given that specific title was St John, in order to distinguish him from St John the Baptist. The feast day of St John the Evangelist is December 27th. However, because of its closeness to Christmas, he is also often remembered on the alternative feast of St John before the Latin Gate, on May 6th. It is very tempting to want to say that we may know the day of the church's consecration, if not the year – but this would be to run well beyond the evidence. Considerable problems remain with the rest of the inscription.

Taking, for example, the second line - ***STITIT HANC*** looks to be a plausible reading (though why is the third ***T*** different to all the others?). However, the word could equally well be incomplete, and have originally been something like ***CONSTITI(T)***, which could be the past tense of either of the verb ***consto***, meaning to agree, to correspond or, equally well, of ***consisto***, meaning to stop, to take a stand. Perhaps, one day, someone with sufficient paleographical skills may make more sense of it, but for now it remains a tantalising enigma.

One useful addition that William Rendle makes to our knowledge is to provide our only information about what happened to the stone afterwards. "In 1733 this stone was in the hands of the clerk of St Thomas's; afterwards it was with the Rev. Jno. Lewis, of Margate, and so mutilated that the letters could be with difficulty made out." Nothing is known beyond this but, if the stone was becoming illegible and had become detached from its place of origin, there would be no continuing reason to preserve it.

Who knows if the unrecognised remains may not be incorporated in some East Kentish rockery or garden wall? The stone has passed out of history, and only this puzzling piece of lettering remains.

THE EARLY CLERGY

St George's, like many parish churches in England, has a tablet fixed to the wall listing the names of Rectors of the parish through the ages. Such a list suggests a continuity of records and tradition. At the same time, it also prompts many questions. Why were there three different Rectors in 1451 and 1470? Did Thomas Profete really hold the office for 58 years, from 1370 to 1428? What was the relationship between the two John Cutlers, who followed one another between 1564 and 1615? And why do two people appear to go under an alias?

We need to recognise that, for the medieval period, such a list is made up from a scattering of chance records that happen to survive. A long gap may simply indicate a lack of information. The single date given for any Rector may be that of his appointment, or of the end of his tenure, or of some point in between – depending on an isolated scrap of evidence.

The most important sources for compiling such lists are the Registers of Diocesan bishops. These began to be kept from the fourteenth century, and many still survive. They were used to record a whole variety of information: licences, legal decisions, institutions and consecrations, appointments and investigations. Sometimes a person may just appear in a list of names – for an ordination, for taxation, or as witness to a document; on other occasions there may be more detailed records, often where there was some problem, or legal dispute.

THE EARLIEST NAMES

No name appears on the list for the first century and a half of the parish's existence. No record has survived naming anyone as Rector. However, there are scraps of information to be found. Martha Carlin, in her 1996 book on *Medieval Southwark,* offers a rather fuller list of 'Rectors and Priests' than the one that is usually copied. (1) In particular, she draws attention to two names to be found in early documents, which pre-date the name of Martin, as Rector in 1245.

The first of these appears in a manuscript dated to between the years 1144 – 1150. The Public Record Office holds a number of ancient deeds amongst its Exchequer documents. Some of these relate to property in Southwark belonging to the bishopric of Winchester, including an agreement between Bermondsey Priory and Henry, Bishop of Winchester, about the acquisition of the lands on which Winchester Palace was later built, on Bankside. The document – a single, folded sheet of parchment, in good condition, - has five separate sections. One of a number of names added to the last part of the document is ***Rob'tus sacerdos de sto. georgio*** – 'Robert, priest of St George's'. Because he is just described as 'priest' he cannot positively be added to the list of Rectors, though that may have been his role. (2)

There has been some debate, among historians, about whether the acquisition of parishes by monastic houses might have affected the pattern of ministry. Did one of the monks of Bermondsey walk down Long Lane to preside at the altar of St George's in the 1100s, or would the Priory have engaged a secular priest to look after the church? Perhaps Robert's involvement as a witness to this transaction, involving Priory lands, suggests that the link remained a close one.

The truth is that we know all too little of parish life and ministry at this period for any secure pronouncement to be made. A priest would certainly be required to say Mass, but neither marriage nor confession before a priest had yet become as regularised as they would be in the following centuries. Children would have needed to be baptised, but often this might have been done at large corporate ceremonies, at Easter or Whitsun. (3) One recent writer suggests that the shift from ethnic names to biblical ones during this period, may imply the influence of parish priests. In general, however, "very little is known about the service of most English churches in the years around 1100." (4)

There is one other isolated reference, from a date more than half a century before continuous records begin. The Calendar of Patent Rolls for the reign of Henry III has an entry for 1241 which reads "Presentation of Ralph de Dunion/Dunton (?) to the church of St Gregory, Sutwerk, in the kings gift by reason of the voidance of the bishopric of Winchester; directed to the official of the archdeacon of Surrey." As there was no known church of St Gregory in Southwark, at any period, it is a reasonable guess that this is a mistake for St George.

If Ralph Dunton was presented as Rector of St George's, however, he cannot have been there long. It is only four years later that the first specific reference to a Rector is to be found, among the ancient records of St Thomas Hospital. At this early stage the hospital was still attached to the church of St Thomas in Southwark. Among their collection of charters and other records of gifts, the following is to be found:

> *Grant by Master Martin, Rector of St George's Church, Southwark, and Nicholas, chaplain of the same, executors of the will of Ralph Carbunell, of 2s. a year rent to the said Hospital, which the said Ralph bequeathed to the Hospital out of his tenement in Trenetlane.*
> *Seal of William, son and heir of the said Ralph.*
> *Feast of All Souls, 1245.* (5)

This does not tell us about the beginning or end of Martin's time as Rector, only that he was in post in 1254. He had, presumably, had time to become sufficiently well trusted to be taken as the executor of someone's will. It also tells us that he had at least one other ordained person on the parish staff.

DISPUTES AND ALIASES

More substantial information starts to become available with the earliest of the Bishop's Registers. Southwark was for much of its history within the Diocese of Winchester. It is within the registers of Bishop Woodlock (1305–16) that we find our next information, and learn a little more about the incumbency of William de Alyngio. On September 30th 1307 the Bishop issued a Commission to settle a dispute about the presentation to St George's, Southwark. (6)

William de Alyngio had been nominated by the Prior and monks of Bermondsey as the new Rector. However, his appointment was disputed by a certain Peter of St James. It sounds as though Peter was in possession of the church and refusing to give it up. Perhaps he had already been ministering at St George's, like Nicholas the chaplain, half a century before, and thought he should have been made Rector. The sub-prior of St Mary, Southwark and master Henry of Derby are charged to look into the matter, and Peter of St James is to be required to substantiate his claim.

Apparently Peter was not able to uphold his case and William de Alyngio became the new Rector. Within the year, however, we find the bishop granting him a licence to go off and study for two years. It was not unusual for medieval bishops to grant leave for this kind of 'in-service training', which often involved study at a university. For a promising young man from a humble background, study at university might only be possible once they were able to use income from their benefice to maintain themselves. It has been remarked though, that "the bishops appear to have had no means of finding out whether the rector really diligently pursued his studies or merely enjoyed a holiday..." (7)

William may have benefited from his studies, but it does look as if they caused him to take his mind off some of his continuing obligations to the parish and the diocese. In 1309 the bishop issued a mandate to the Archdeacon of Surrey to raise certain sums long overdue for payment by rectors and vicars in his archdeaconry, and to cite the defaulters for contumacy. The list of defaulters included St George, Southwark – along with St Mary Magdalene, Bermondsey and St Mary, Rotherhithe. (8)

In 1315, following the resignation of William, Alard de Alyngio was appointed to succeed him as Rector. The coincidence of the names suggests that they were from the same place and possibly related – though we have no way now of knowing what the connection between them might have been.

Also from this period, we find some figures relating to taxation. In a list of 'Crown Dues' the figure of £2.0.0. is set beside the 'parson of the church of St George' in 1303, and 13s. 4d. in 1309. From 1309 there is a certificate to William, relating to the collection of first fruits on benefices that have fallen vacant in the five years previous. The figure given here is ten marks with pension. (9) This corresponds to figures in the *valor* of Edward 1, taken in 1292, which has the benefice of St George's rated at 10 marks, and states that it paid a pension of 20s. to the Abbot of Bermondsey. (10)

Alard was Rector for less than three years. In the year 1317/18, in the Register of Bishop Sandale, we learn of the appointment of William de Halybourn. Nothing else is known of William, though a Grant of land, among the records of St Thomas Hospital, dated 1329, defines the southern boundary of the property in question as the 'tenement of William, Parson of the Church of St George.' He remained in post for nearly 30 years, until he died. (11)

On 20th February, 1349, Everard de Pratellis was admitted to fill his place. In 1352 Everard was granted a licence 'to be at the service of Mary, countess of Pembroke' though he continued as Rector of St George's until October 1362. (12) An entry in Bishop Edington's Register for that date records the 'Examination of an Exchange by commission of the bishop, as between Thomas de Mottyng, perpetual vicar of Camberwell and Everard Volet, rector of the church of St George, Southwark.'

This is the first instance of an 'alias', where the records contain a major variation of the name of what clearly seems to be the same person. Perhaps *de Pratellis* signified his place of origin while *Volet* was a surname. The term 'alias' suggests, to modern ears, something a little shifty. Here it merely tells us that the same person appears to be signified under more than one version of his name. Surnames were not fully fixed or hereditary at the period, but were still in formation. Their use seems to have spread from the aristocracy downwards, and to have become standardised with the increase of written records.

The exchange of posts between Everard and Thomas de Mottyng was not unusual, and we shall come across another instance soon. (13) Although Thomas is certainly recorded as the next rector of St George's, there is no corresponding record in the list of vicars of St Giles, Camberwell.

Nothing more is known of Thomas Mottyng, except that he died in post, probably in 1369. (14)

THOMAS PROFETE

In January 1369/70 Thomas Profete was instituted as rector on the death of' Mottyng. Profete was not appointed by Bermondsey Priory, the regular patrons of the parish, but by the king, "in whose hands the temporals of Bermondsey Priory were by reason of war with France." (15) The king in question would have been Edward III, and the Hundred Years War was well under way by this time.

It would appear that Thomas Profete had not yet been ordained when he was appointed Rector of St George's. He was one of a group of men who were made deacons by the Bishop of Winchester, at Farnham Castle on 9th March 1370. In June of the same year the Bishop of Winchester issued 'letters dimissory' authorising the Bishop of London to ordain him as priest, which he did on June 8th. This was not unusual practice at the time. (16)

It is possible that Thomas Profete may have been someone who had gained recognition in the king's administration and who was being rewarded with this appointment. More specifically, he may have been a protégé of William of Wykeham, the bishop of the diocese. Wykeham was Bishop of Winchester from 1366 to 1404. Although of quite humble origin, he had proved his ability in public service and, being employed by the king on tasks of increasing responsibility, he had become, at this time, one of the most powerful men in the land. From 1367 to 1371 he was Chancellor of England, and Froissart, the contemporary chronicler, wrote that "all things were done by him and without him nothing was done". It has been said that, at this period, "Edward was becoming increasingly dependant on Wykeham's advice in such matters as ecclesiastical preferments". (17)

It appears that Thomas Profete was presented to another benefice – that of SS. Simon & Jude at Norwich, just four months before he was admitted to St George's. It is not clear how long he retained this. (18) Profete may well have been a promising young man, who was now being rewarded with benefice income, and was also someone who the Chancellor wanted to keep in his own diocese. The 1360s seem to have been a period of high recruitment into the ordained ministry. One study relates this to the effects of the Black Death. The plague may have created an unusual number of job opportunities, thus encouraging more candidates. It may also be that many of those fortunate enough to have survived were left with a greater openness to spiritual concerns. (19)

In December 1378 Thomas was given leave of absence from his parish to go and study at Oxford for two years. (20) This does suggest that he may have been relatively young, when appointed, and was still developing his capabilities. The university at Oxford was well established by this time, and both King Edward and Bishop Wykeham were generous benefactors. It had a high reputation for work in mathematics and astronomy. In theology, fourteenth century Oxford had seen a succession of some of the best minds in Europe – Duns Scotus, William of Ockham, Thomas Bradwardine – but in the 1470s it was dominated by controversy around the radical teaching of John Wyclif.

Wyclif, under the powerful protection of John of Gaunt, developed a body of ideas that challenged many aspects of the contemporary Church and its teaching, and argued in favour of radical reform. His Lollard followers have been seen as forerunners of the Protestant Reformation, a century and a half later. Wyclif's teachings were condemned in the 1380s, but the Oxford attended by Thomas Profete would still have been in ferment around these issues.

Theological unrest, however, was soon to be overtaken by political turmoil. Edward III had died in 1377, and it was during the minority of his grandson, Richard II, that the kingdom was shaken by the upheaval of the Peasant's Revolt. In June 1381, Wat Tyler led his rebel force to camp on Blackheath, and from there moved down into Southwark. They broke open the Marshalsea Prison, and destroyed one of the houses of the marshal. Then, after burning administrative records of the archbishop at Lambeth Palace, they stormed London Bridge to enter the City.

Although the Marshalsea was a little further up the High Street at this time – nearer to the end of what is now Newcomen Street - the rebels may well have come up Kent Street and around St George's on their way there. The church would have seemed to be beset by rioters.

Once the revolt was quelled, there must have been reconstruction work needed in Southwark. It was also during the incumbency of Thomas Profete that St George's church

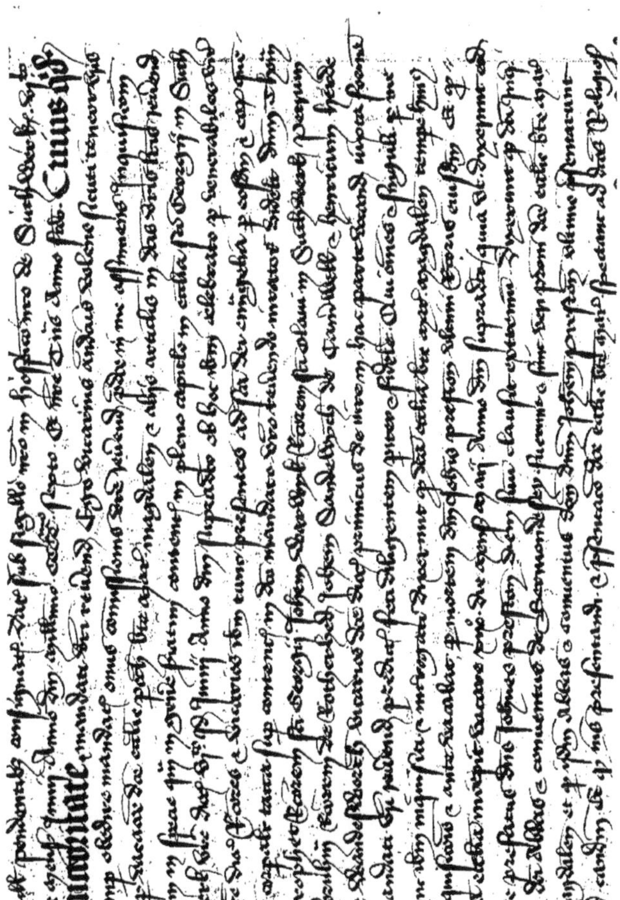

Opposite: Register of Bishop Henry Beaufort, part of folio 27 recto, summoning Thomas Profete and other local clergy to the inquisition in 1406. *(Original in Hampshire Record Office)*

was rebuilt for the first time, ten years after the great uprising.

Perhaps, as with the recent re-construction works, that rebuilding took place against a background of local 'regeneration'? We can be sure that Profete was still in post, from an entry in the Bishop's Register for March 1392, granting him the administration of the effects of a man called Robert Parker, who had died intestate 'in the house of Matilda Solaas in the parish of St George, Southwark.' (21)

Indeed, he was still in post as rector of the church in June 1406. By this time Bishop Wykeham had finally died, and the new Bishop, Henry, Cardinal Beaufort, was holding an inquisition locally. 'Thomas Prophet, Rector of St George's', is one of the names listed in connection with this. (22)

This eventful period was also one in which Southwark became a centre of literary activity. It is the era of Chaucer's *Canterbury Pilgrims,* who meet one April at the Tabard Inn (at what is now Talbot Yard in the Borough High Street) before setting off on their journey. The inns of Southwark would have been the starting point for many such groups. Although Chaucer does not mention St George's, we can well imagine that the church might have offered a convenient point at which to pause and say a prayer, or light a candle, before they started down the road to Kent.

There is a more direct link, however, with Chaucer's contemporary, John Gower. Gower wrote works of poetry in all three of the literary languages of time – French, Latin and English. For the last 30 years of his life he lived in the priory of St Mary Overie, what is now Southwark Cathedral. His splendid tomb, in red and green and gold, remains as a prominent feature in the north aisle there, where he lies with his head resting on the three principle books for which he was known. He was a generous benefactor of the Priory, but when he died in 1408 he also remembered St George's church among his bequests. It seems reasonable to assume that he must sometimes have visited the church and worshipped there, retaining some affection for it. Presumably its Rector would have been among his acquaintances.

Beyond this point, we move into an area of uncertainty. The Bishop's Registers for the years 1415 to 1446 are lost. As there is no record of a new appointment to St George's before they cease, it is possible that Thomas Profete remained as rector until 1415. This would have extended his tenure to some 45 years and, even if he was appointed as a young man, must have made him around 70 years old.

THE LAWYERS

A man called William Brooke is listed as being in post in 1428, but whether he succeeded Thomas Profete, or whether anyone else came between them, it is not possible to say. (23) Nor do we know when William Brooke's incumbency might have come to an end. The next sure information is from the first register of William Waynflete, who became Bishop of Winchester in 1447.

When the records resume, the parish seems to have moved into a whole new era. One commentator, writing about pluralism and absenteeism in the period before the Reformation, singles out this parish for comment, saying that St George's, Southwark, "...was a favourite living for courtiers and officials with little opportunity, and perhaps less inclination, to serve the cure of souls personally." (24). He lists six different Rectors, who held the living at some point during the next 100 years, as fitting this description.

The first of these was Master William Hoper, doctor of law, who on 7th April 1450 was presented to the parish church of St George of Southwark, vacant through the death of Master Robert Amyas. It is possible that Robert Amyas may have been a seventh name to add to the list. We know nothing about the length of time he was rector, but it may well be – given the rather unusual name – that he can be identified with a Robert Amyas who studied canon law Oxford in the 1440s and was in priest's orders by 1449. (25)

William Hooper was an experienced lawyer, who must have been in his 50s, if not older, when he briefly held the living of St George's. He was a doctor of both Civil and Canon Law, and had acted as commissioner in appeal from the court of the King's Audience, and the court of Admiralty. He had also held a long list of benefices and other church preferments, changing them often enough to suggest that his concern was more to do with their commercial value than with the cure of souls. He held the living of St George's for a matter of months only, before exchanging with another man. It seems unlikely that he could have had anything but a cursory acquaintance with the parish itself. (26)

The medieval parish was important as an economic unit. The collection of tithes was a principal mechanism by which agricultural surplus was turned into a means of support for other sections of society. One writer suggests that "In some sense, the rector is best considered a manager who could but certainly need not have direct involvement with the spiritual care of his parishioners....He managed the economic resources of the parish, economic resources that were often as significant as those that went to the lord of the manor." (27) These resources included the tithe/tenth of parish produce, as well as sole benefit from glebe lands belonging to the church, and various fees and offerings. In return he was liable for taxation and repair of the chancel of the church, as well as providing for actual ministry to the parish. Although St George's was an urban parish, it would have income from other financial assets, property and rentals for instance, in place of agricultural produce.

We have already seen how a rector could use the income from the parish to further his studies at university, and how he might come to the post because of his administrative skills. The medieval clergy, who could read and write, provided a significant part of what we might call the 'civil service'. The management of their agricultural parish might be farmed out to a bailiff. After the period of the 'Black Death' the practice of leasing a parish became more common: "…rectors and perpetual vicars leased out parishes and treated them as an organised business endeavour that included the religious services and obligations." (28) The lease might be to a small consortium of people, which could include one party who was in orders and who would take on the parish ministry as his share of the investment.

There is a long entry in Bishop Waynflete's register recording the exchange of livings between Hooper and Rowland Barnes, of Ikcombe in Worcester diocese (now Icomb in Gloucester) (29) This is dated 15th August 1451. Hooper was to hold Icomb for less than two years. Rowland Barnes was at St George's for an even shorter time, but for a different reason. There is no indication that he was one of the university trained lawyers, but even if he did intend to live in the parish, he had little opportunity to do so. He must have died within barely a year of taking up this new appointment. It is on 13th November 1452 that Master Roger Potter, also called Redonall, is presented by Bermondsey Priory as the new rector of St George's, 'vacant through the death of Rowland Banes, the last rector'. (30)

From what little evidence there is, neither Roger Potter/Redonall, nor his successor, a man called Thomas Candour, fit obviously into the succession of university educated men in public service. Between them, they occupy the post for a period of 18 years, though the date at which the one succeeded the other is not evident. In 1470, however, Thomas Candour resigned the living, initiating another period of rapid change.

In April 1470, Willam Moggys was appointed to succeed him. Moggys had spent many years at Oxford, where he had been a Junior Proctor and a collector of University rents, as well as a student. He was already in his 40s when he was admitted as Rector of St George's. Like William Hooper before him, he held the living for only a few months. On the first day of August, of the same year, Master John Fox, Doctor of Letters, was appointed, following the free resignation of William Moggys. His main living appears to have been at Hartlebury, in Worcester diocese, where he was eventually buried. (31)

John Fox seems to have come originally from Yorkshire. He had studied Civil and Canon Law, achieving a doctorate in 1457. His student days were not without incident. In 1456 he was convicted of bearing arms, and only released from prison upon payment of a fine. This did not prevent him from enjoying a successful career, which included holding one archdeaconry, two canonries and at least four prebends. He was rector of St George's for seven years.

Dr John Fox resigned the living in October 1477. Another Canon lawyer, called John Brown, was appointed 1482. (32) Brown's appointment to St George's happened in the same year that he became a Clerk in Chancery, and one is inclined to suspect that the latter post may have been the one that occupied most of his time. He lived till 1500, but did not hold the living of St George's for the whole of that time, as we shall see shortly. (33)

For the five years in between Fox and Brown, however, the post was held by a man of rather different status, who seems to inaugurate a new phase in the life of the parish.

THE COURTIERS: THE POPE'S COLLECTOR

Between the names of John Fox and John Brown, the list of Rectors of St George's usually carries the name 'John Gylis'. I assumed that I was looking for a similar figure, a university educated lawyer, who held the living for five years, in plurality with several others, to help pay him for his legal services elsewhere. However, I could not, at first, find anyone corresponding to that name, or any likely variant of it. Going back to search again, however, it finally emerged that the name 'John Gylis' concealed the true identity of a rather different kind of person. The next Rector of St George's was actually an Italian, called Giovanni Gigli – who was sent to England from Rome as Papal Collector, in 1477, and ended his career as Bishop of Worcester.

Gigli's name seems to have caused some difficulty to the English. More than a dozen known variants of it are recorded, some as remote as *Liliis, Zilio* or even *Sighs.* (34) What has happened in the case of St George's is not too difficult to work out. The most common way his name was written in England was *Giglis*. The clerk who was writing up the Bishop's Register - copying, perhaps, from notes he had been sent - changed 'Giovanni' to its English equivalent 'John', a reasonable enough emendation. It then only required him to mistake a – perhaps hastily written – 'ig' for 'y', and the Italian cleric had been transformed into 'John Giles'. (35).

Giovanni Gigli was born in 1434. Although his parents were native to the Italian city of Lucca, he was actually born in Bruges, where his father Carlo was carrying on business as a merchant. He may have been in England as a youth, since a record survives of a safe-conduct being granted to his father to trade in England in 1451. (36).

Giovanni trained as a lawyer, and was a Doctor of Civil and Canon Law. Having made his way up in the papal service, he was sent to England as the Collector of papal revenues here. His letters of denization are recorded on 12th December 1477 (37) However, he had already been made Rector of St George's, Southwark, by that date. His admission as Rector is recorded as 24th October of that year. It appears that he must have been granted the living, more or less on his arrival, as part of the means of providing for himself.

The post of Papal Collector was held by a series of learned Italian scholars and writers through this period. The post offered a certain status, in a society where the benefits of a humanist education were much appreciated. However, it has been suggested that "the duties of the office were probably more depressing than onerous." (38) Payment of taxes to the Holy See was, in effect, largely voluntary, and not many volunteered. One of Gigli's successors wrote back to Rome in 1515, saying, "As for Peter's Pence, there are few who wish to pay it...I cannot send you what I do not receive." (39) Only the fees that had to be paid, to secure a post or obtain a dispensation, could be relied upon. Nevertheless, the Pope may have considered it 'an economical way of providing for an ambassador.' (40)

Just how difficult the job could be was something that Gigli found out for himself in 1480, when he appeared before a synod of clergy in London, to ask for financial help for the Pope, in his efforts to raise a crusade for the defence of Rhodes against the Turks. For all the Collector's eloquence, pleading that the Pope had sold his jewels and melted down his plate to provide for this cause, no money was forthcoming from the English clergy. (41)

Fortunately for Gigli, he was soon prospering in other ways. During the next twenty years, he was made a canon or prebendary of eight different English cathedrals, as well as being given two Archdeaconries and becoming Rector of several other parishes. At the same time, he was also making himself useful to the king.

WRITER AND DIPLOMAT

One of the ways in which Giovanni Gigli commended himself was through demonstrating his skills in writing. The new learning of Italian humanism was challenging medieval scholarship, at this time, not only by shifting the basis of thought, but also with changes of literary style. Humanist scholars went back to models from before the Middle Ages, deriving their Latin style from the ancient orator, Cicero. Their penmanship was derived from what they took to be a classical mode, though it was actually based on lettering of the early medieval Carolingian period. The effect in both areas was something that seemed altogether clearer and more elegant. These new cultural fashions were brought into England during this period, and figures like Gigli, and his successor Carmelianus, were in the forefront of this movement.

There is a finely written and illustrated manuscript book, now in the British Library, which contains works by Gigli, presumably in his own hand. (42) The book was apparently a gift to Richard Fox, Bishop of Winchester, who was one of the most powerful men in the land In the letter that opens his book, Gigli refers to Fox as 'Maecenas', which certainly implies that he had either received patronage from him, or had good reason to expect to do so. (43)

Gigli's book contains a prose work on some questions of church law, followed by several poems. The longest of the poems is an *Epithalamium*, written to celebrate the marriage of Henry VII to Elizabeth of York, which signalled the end of the Wars of the Roses and the beginning of a new dynasty. Gigli had already played a role in obtaining the necessary dispensations from Rome, allowing this marriage to go ahead. (44)

It appears that Gigli was able to make himself useful to the Crown right from the beginning of his career in England. Already, in 1479, Edward IV employed him as a member of a mission sent to Rome to discuss a peace treaty being made with Charles VIII of France. The later part of his career, during the reign of Henry VII, was increasingly taken up with diplomatic work, and he was mainly resident in Rome from 1490, as ambassador and orator for English interests.

His services must have been valued by the king. In 1497 he was appointed Bishop of Worcester, and his consecration took place in Rome. As it turned out, he was never to visit his diocese, as he died the following year, still in Rome, and was buried in the church of the English hospice there. A letter surviving from 1498, part of a correspondence between Henry

VII and the Duke of Milan, shows that Henry was also trying hard to get Gigli appointed as a Cardinal. The brother of the Duke, Cardinal Ascanio Sforza, has been persuaded to help further his cause. (45) However, it was all too late.

Gigli was Rector of St George's for just five years, and it is hard to think that, with all his other involvements, the parish found much place in his thoughts. Like other Rectors of the period, he would have employed assistant clergy to carry out the parish ministry, and may hardly have visited the place himself. Nevertheless, we can establish that the interests of St George's were not wholly neglected by him, and that he did take some trouble to provide for its needs.

LETTER OF INDULGENCE

Printed copies survive of a Letter of Indulgence, issued in Rome, and promising spiritual benefits to those who make gifts for the repair and maintenance of St George's Church. The printed copies all date from the early 1500s, and the incumbency of his Italian successor. However, the original date of issue of the Indulgence itself has been dated to 1479. It was approved by a group of Cardinals, whose names appear in the text of the Letter. The coincidence of that particular group makes it possible to pinpoint the date. 1479 is a time when we can securely place Gigli in Rome, on business for King Edward IV.

Selling indulgences, which promised remission of time spent in Purgatory, had become a favoured method of fund-raising during this period, and the new technology of the printing press allowed for their mass production and more intensive distribution. Gigli, from his work as Collector of Papal revenues, would have been well-versed in their use, and it is known that he employed William Caxton to print indulgences for him in support of the Pope's planned crusade, in 1481, and again in 1489. It may well be that he also put the indulgence for St George's into circulation, though the surviving evidence is only of its continuing use twenty years later. Either way, the parish would have derived some benefit from the short incumbency of one of its more exalted Rectors.

PETER CARMELIANUS

Giovanni Gigli must have resigned as Rector of St George's by 1482, as that was the year in which the lawyer John Brown was admitted. Brown held the living for seven or eight years, and was replaced in 1490. The new Rector, Peter Carmelianus, as an Italian, a Humanist scholar, and a courtier, was a man much more in the mould of Gigli – though his early life had followed a different course. (46) There was, in fact, a very direct link between the two, as we shall see.

Very little is known of his early years. He was born in the town of Brescia in 1451, and travelled quite widely in Europe before coming to England in 1482. Here he set about trying to commend himself through his literary skills. He had some initial success with a long poem addressed to the Prince of Wales, for which he was rewarded. Unluckily for him, the king died shortly after this, and the prince in question – briefly Edward V - was one of the two murdered in the Tower, to make way for the succession of their uncle, Richard III.

Having lost that source of patronage, Carmelianus did make one attempt to ingratiate himself by sending copies of a new poem to members of Richard's establishment. Nothing seems to have come of this and he took himself off to Oxford, where he did editorial work for a printer called Theodoric Rood.

The overthrow of Richard III at the battle of Bosworth gave him a fresh opportunity to try and find a place in the royal service. We have seen how Giovanni Gigli produced a poem in celebration of the marriage of Henry VII and Elizabeth of York; Carmelianus was to do the same, to good effect, on the occasion of the birth of the royal couple's first son, Arthur. Within days of the presentation of this poem he received from the king a pension which "he that shall be next promoted to the bishopric of Worcester is bound to yield to a clerk of ours at our nomination." The person 'next promoted to the bishopric of Worcester' was Robort Morton, who was then Master of the Rolls. There is evidence Carmelianus had been doing work at Rolls House, so we can glimpse the connections of patronage.

It is almost certain that he was also receiving help from his predecessor at St George's, Giovanni Gigli. The first page of the manuscript book containing Gigli's writings is taken up with a letter addressed to Richard Fox, for whom the book seems to have been intended. Fox was close to Henry VII from the start of his reign, having joined him when he was still in exile. He became a member of the king's council, as well as Secretary, Keeper of the Privy Seal, and bishop successively of Exeter, Bath and Wells, Durham and finally Winchester. The letter, probably dating from the beginning of 1487, mentions *'noster Carmelianus'* – 'our Carmelianus'. The implication of this familiar epithet is that Carmelianus was well known to both of them, and was probably acting as some sort of go-between.

This combination of friends in high places, together with his own skills, soon helped to secure him the further reward of a 'grant in consideration of good and diligent service...of a pension within the king's monastery of Hyde.' (47)

It may seem odd to us now that church revenues should be used to pay people in the employment of the state. However, the late medieval church was the best resourced institution in the land. Also, it had traditionally provided most of the men of learning and administrative skill. The word 'clerk' reminds us that someone who could write well was once synonymous with someone in holy orders. There were many of these historic pensions and other incomes, often with little or no work attached, which could be used to reward useful servants of the Crown.

AT ST GEORGE'S

At this stage Carmelianus was not a 'clergyman', as we would think of it, and had no need to be one in order to receive these particular gifts. However, he must now have reached a stage where, if he was to continue and advance in the king's service and to profit significantly from it, he would need to be in a position to receive richer ecclesiastical livings. It would not be unduly cynical, at this period, to suppose that his decision to take orders in his late thirties was more to do with career development than any sudden sense of vocation.

He may have been admitted to the minor orders – janitor, lector, exorcist and acolyte – at the time of his education in Italy. These singled out a man as a 'clerk', offering some privileges, without the requirement of commitments such as celibacy. Those pursuing an academic career would often stop at that stage. Now, in 1489, he was ordained Sub-deacon at St Paul's in April, and Deacon in June. (48) His Title – that is the source of his maintenance (usually a specific appointment) – is given, on both occasions as '£10 per annum of his patrimony'. Presumably this means that he was to provide for himself out of the church revenues he was already receiving. When he was ordained Priest, however, in April 1490, it is given as 'St George in Southwerk'. (49) His educational status is recorded as 'Magister'.

Further confirmation of his appointment as rector of St George's from 1490 can be found in a collection of Papal letters. This reads,

"To Peter Carmelianus, rector of the parish church of St George in Suthwerke, diocese of Winchester, dispensation – at his supplication – to receive and retain for life together with the above parish church, one other....." (50)

From time to time, over the centuries, the church has tried to set limits on people holding several offices at once, as a means of increasing their income. At other times, though, for one reason or another, church authorities have readily colluded in the practice of 'pluralism'. Here Carmelianus is given permission to hold St George's along with one other living. In fact he would go on adding to the church offices he held for many years to come. (51)

We might want to ask what was there about St George's that made it an appropriate benefice to bestow on figures of this sort? Southwark, at the end of the fifteenth century, was an area with a rising population. Some of the grand properties which had lined the river bank were beginning to be subdivided, and sometimes turned over to commercial uses. However, these pressures had not yet reached the southern end of the High Street. Although new alleys like the *Mermaid* and the *Blue-eyed Maid* first appear in this period, and the Kings Bench Prison lay just north of the church, St George's Fields still opened out to the south. On the west side of the street, opposite the church, stood the house of the Brandon family, and behind that the Bishop of Winchester's park, with its driveway running along the line of Redcross Way.

The Brandons held the office of Marshal of the Kings Bench prison, from the middle of the fifteenth century. Martha Carlin relates that, "Sir Thomas Brandon, who inherited Brandon Place from his mother in 1497, created a private park adjoining it from some 48 acres of meadows and pastures belonging to the bishop of Winchester." (52) In 1510 the property and the post of marshal passed to his nephew Charles. Charles Brandon was a close companion of the young Henry VIII. He was made Duke of Suffolk in 1514, and was able to marry the king's own sister, Mary, in 1515. From 1516 he acquired other adjacent properties and rebuilt the house on a grand scale, as befitted his elevated situation.

The panorama drawn by the artist Wyngaerde in the 1540s shows the house as a very elaborate structure, with decorated towers and pinnacles, set behind a gatehouse opposite the church. Henry VIII himself was later to acquire the house, now known as Suffolk Place, exchanging it with Brandon for another property. There is no evidence of Henry spending much time there himself, but in 1537 he granted it to his last wife, Jane Seymour. (53)

What we see is that, for more than half a century, the area immediately around St George's was regarded as a suitable place of residence for court favourites and for members of the royal family. Perhaps this is what made a rising courtier seem an appropriate choice as Rector. Any occasional visits he made to the parish may have been timed to coincide with the presence of distinguished guests in residence at Suffolk Place. Perhaps it was a fashionable place to worship on April 23rd, the feast day of England's patron saint, to whom the church was dedicated. During this period the church had an active fraternity of St George, and charitable donations were sought to maintain the priests who said daily masses there. (54)

COURT POET

To earn the revenues bestowed on him by the king, Peter Carmelianus had a role as a court poet, and soon was to be given the post of Latin Secretary to the king. Carmelianus had not been the only writer to produce a poem in celebration of the birth of Prince Arthur. Giovanni Gigli had also written one, so had Bernard André, another scholar with a continental background. (55) They were all part of a circle of scholarly writers, on whose skills the king could call, when required.

One of the information boards in St George's church describes Carmelianus as 'Poet Laureate', and this term does occur in connection with his writings. However, we should not confuse it with the office that exists today, and which did not come into being in its present form until a century and a half after his time. This was not some clearly designated office that he held. In fact, he is already describing himself as *'Poetae Laureati'* to Prince Edward in 1482, when he had no position at court, only his first small taste of royal patronage.

The role of a Tudor court poet was likely to be as much about shaping state propaganda as about writing celebratory odes.

This role is well illustrated by an incident in 1489, which brought court poets into front line action on behalf of the state. England and France were in confrontation over the future of Brittany, which had remained largely independent of the French crown. Henry felt a personal obligation to the Bretons, who had sheltered him in exile, but he did not have the will or the capacity to engage in an expensive war that he was unlikely to win. Instead he engaged in a prolonged diplomatic campaign, to distract the French.

During 1489, two high-ranking French embassies were sent to London. The negotiations dragged on, never reaching a conclusion. After they left, Robert Gaguin, one of the leading members of the French embassy, himself a distinguished scholar and writer, gave vent to his frustrations in a poem. His short piece complains of wasted efforts, blames the English for ingratitude and pretence, and accuses the king of preparing for a war he cannot win. (56)

This demanded a response, and the English court poets were called into action. Several replies were penned, not all of which have survived. However, it seems that Carmelianus was thought to have hit the mark most effectively. His colleague Bernard André later wrote, in his Life of Henry VII, "Next, master Pietro Carmeliano of Brescia, a most renowned poet and orator and indeed a most meritorious royal secretary, in a most elegant poem, which I was not able to obtain as I was writing this, on account of his absence, pummelled Gaguin remarkably, who was by turns reviled and mocked."

It is difficult for us now to recover a feel for the wit and sharpness of the poem, which so impressed contemporaries. What comes across more strongly is the belligerent tone of Carmelianus' response.

> The English attend meeting after meeting
> with the French, searching for peace
> on honourable terms. The Frank says 'Non!'
> Mad lust for domination rules out an accord.

His words speak peace, his deeds bare cruel claws;
his tongue cannot keep tune with the heart.
Why pick a fight? Can you not grasp,
vain Frank, that stout strong Britons come out top?
Everyone knows the French have only ever won
by cheating and lies, foul-play and trickery.
You turn your weapons on our allies,
subject the Breton land to your harsh yoke.
You affront an unprotected virgin, orphan princess,
grabbing at 'rights' you never had in law.
Justly we defend a people bound to us
by treaty. This is true-hearted work.
Wrong-headedness has got a grip on you,
and harsh lust grips you too. Back off,
if you have any sense; let sleeping lions lie,
lest their dire strength should wake to overcome your own.
England, you seek peace in vain; waste no more time.
To arms! Only a vanquished Frenchman sues for peace.

In the end the French king had his way over Brittany. Nevertheless, Henry had asserted English influence across the Channel, and avoided the appearance of colluding in the end of Breton independence. He may well have been content at having avoided the expense of a war, whilst returning French fire at the cost of no more than ink and parchment. The timing of this exchange does suggest the possibility that the gift of the living of St George's might even have been a reward for literary exertions in defence of English pride. (57)

How good a poet was Carmelianus? All his work was written in Latin, so it is hard to judge without being fluent in that language. However, those who have taken it on themselves to comment are not particularly flattering. Gardiner says, "From the first he shows himself to be a court poet and nothing more..." (58) Even less complimentary is Ricardo Weiss, one of the foremost authorities on Humanist learning. In an unpublished note, he comments on the poem about St Katherine of Alexandria, which Carmelianus wrote during the reign of Richard III, "As for the poem it amounts to nothing more than a short metrical rendering of the facts of the life of

St Catherine....Its only importance is the preface to Brackenbury, since the standard of versification is hardly above that of a clever schoolboy's exercise and the contents of the poems are without any interest at all." (59).

LATIN SECRETARY

Carmelianus acquired another role at court when he was appointed as the King's Latin Secretary. This brought him to a position of greater status and apparent influence. The king's Latin correspondence would include many of his exchanges with other European rulers. Latin remained the language of diplomacy, a *lingua franca* through which the European heads of state could communicate on something like equal terms of understanding. Employing Carmelianus, who could write in a fine modern script and turn polished phrases in the classical style - rather than someone using the Church script and language that was going out of fashion - would have enabled Henry to present a contemporary face to other rulers. (60) It also meant that Carmelianus became party to correspondence treating of high matters of state, and had a hand in the drafting of diplomatic exchanges, finding the best choice of words to ensure that subtle points were rightly understood by their recipients.

He may not himself have been moving the levers of power, but he was seen to be close enough to them for him to become a person worth cultivating, not least by foreign governments. In 1495, the Spanish rulers Ferdinand and Isabella wrote to their ambassador, saying that,

"A letter for Master Pedro [i.e. Peter] the Latin secretary of King Henry is enclosed. Thank him for his services, and promise him favour and money..." (61)

We are given a closer glimpse of Carmelianus at work for the king by some dispatches from the Milanese ambassador Raimondo de Soncino, who was sent to London in 1498. The affairs of Italy took centre stage during this period, as that country suffered a series of invasions and effectively lost its independence to the more centralised European powers. Raimondo writes back to Ludovico Sforza, the duke, reporting his arrival in England and saying that the Genoese, who were looking after him, advised that he should not approach the king without first sending notice to him by a messenger.

"By commission from the King, Carmeliano wrote to him that if his business was important he might come to Woodstock of the 24th inst." (62)
The audience was delayed because, Raimondo believes, Henry is also negotiating with the French. Once his interview does take place, there is the matter of drawing up a communiqué afterwards. The envoy offers to prepare a draft. The king was happy for him to do this, but when he took it to him, "...the King said that although it contained the sense of the reply, he wished it written more fully, and that he would order a draft to be prepared in such form as seemed fitting to him. Accordingly last evening...Messr. Pietro Carmeliano, who had drawn up the minute in his own hand, the King correcting it, delivered the document to him, requesting him, in the King's name, not to alter the words." Raimondo promises to do this, and then copies it verbatim. He encloses the text with his letter, saying that he "would gladly have sent the original, but Pietro Carmeliano said the King chose that it should be returned to him." Henry, it appears, liked to keep his originals on file. (63)

Mention of Carmelianus occurs most frequently in the extensive correspondence with the Venetian Republic, whose territories then included his native city. The documentation is too extensive to deal with in detail here. Suffice it to say that the Venetian authorities must have been delighted to find that their correspondence with the English king was now passing through the hands of one of their own countrymen. Carmelianus writes to the Doge, describing himself as his 'subject', and assuring him that he will demonstrate his zeal for the welfare of Venice. Some of the letters are written in Italian, not in Latin, and are outside of his official correspondence. The implication is that he may be not only

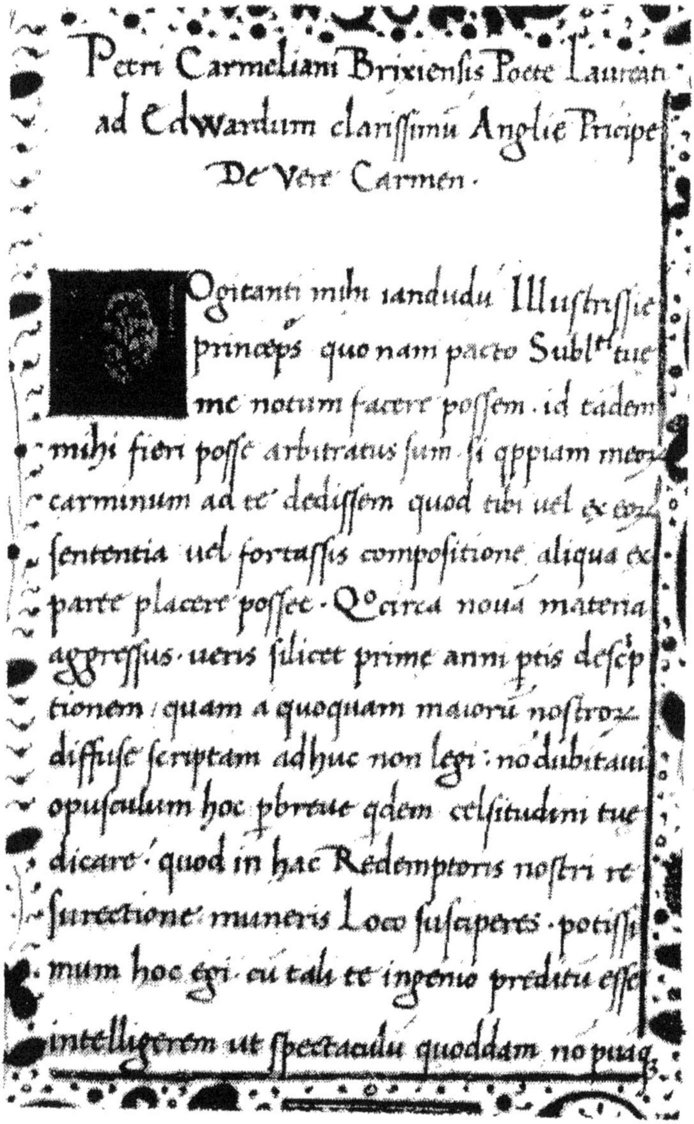
Petri Carmeliani Brixiensis Poete Laureati
ad Edwardum clarissimu Anglie Pricipe
De Vere Carmen.

Cogitanti mihi iandudu Illustrissie
princeps quonam pacto Sublti tue
me notum facere possem. id tadem
mihi fieri posse arbitratus sum si qppiam meo
carminum ad te dedissem quod tibi uel ex eo
sententia uel fortassis compositione aliqua ex
parte placere posset. Quocirca noua materia
aggressus ueris silicet prime anni ptis descp
tionem quam a quoquam maioru nostro
diffuse scriptam adhuc non legi: no dubitaui
opusculum hoc pbreue qdem celsitudini tue
dicare. quod in hac Redemptoris nostri re
surrectione muneris Loco susciperes. potissi
mum hoc egi. cu tali te ingenio preditu esse
intelligerem ut spectaculu quoddam no piuq

Opposite: The hand-writing of Peter Carmelianus. The beginning of his dedication of the poem *De Vere* to Edward, Prince of Wales. Compare this with the previous illustration to get some idea of the change in writing style which scholars like Carmelianus were bringing to the English court.
(B.L. Royal MS 12.A.xxix, fol. 1 recto)

acting as an informant, passing useful information, but also trying to influence English policy to the advantage of Venice.

On one occasion two letters are sent on the same day to the Venetian Consul in London. The first is an official letter of instruction, expressing pleasure at what Carmeliano has communicated to them of the King's goodwill, and especially for his willingness in helping to 'negotiate a good peace' with the Emperor. (64) The second letter is a covering instruction to the Consul. He is to read the first letter word for word to Carmeliano. It would be good if the latter could then arrange for the consul to speak directly to the King – 'in the which case he is to read the King the identical first letter.' "Inform Carmeliano that in the said letter they do not thank Carmeliano for his goodwill and exertions in favour of the Signory, in order that he may, if requisite, read the said letter to the King." The King's response is to be transmitted with the utmost speed, regardless of expense and using cipher for secrecy.

All this has led some commentators to suggest that Carmelianus acted as some sort of double agent. One writes that "...the aspect of Carmelaino's biography that remains least well undertsood is his work as a Venetian agent in England, secret or otherwise." (65)

It is evident that the Venetians valued him At the very least they could be confident of being able to communicate clearly with the English court and have their position well understood and persuasively presented. They also hoped that Carmelianus could exercise some influence on their behalf – whether those hopes were well founded or not. More questionably, they might have had a source of sensitive information, which they might not otherwise receive.

Certainly the surviving correspondence of 1509/10 does suggest that Carmelianus could have been the source through which they received early warning about the League of Cambrai and its hostile intentions. Whether such information was forwarded with or without the knowledge of the King is another matter. Henry VII would have been fully aware of Carmelianus' close links to the Venetians, and may have regarded that as part of his value. Allowing him to forward sensitive intelligence in a private capacity could have been a way of leaking information in a manner that was 'deniable' by the English government.

Carmelianus kept his post as Latin Secretary to the King for a year into the new reign, but not much longer. Henry VII died on 21st April 1509. "Mr Petir Carmelyon the Kings secretary for the Latin tongue" appears among a list of attendants at the funeral, though he does not appear to have been among the clergy who met the body at St George's. (66)

THE NEW REIGN

The letters to and from Venice continue for a while, then one dated 3rd June 1510 comes from Andrea Ammonio, Latin Secretary of Henry VIII. Carmelianus has been replaced. Was this just a change following on the start of the reign – a reshuffle of government jobs under a new administration? Or was there some particular reason for Carmelianus being removed?

During that year the interests of England and Venice moved in different directions. The young king Henry VIII was keen to show his mettle, and there was no better way of doing this than a confrontation with France. At this point, however, the Venetians found it advantageous to switch their policy and ally themselves with the French. One of the last letters received in Venice, written by Carmelianus for the king, "Complains of the league made with the king of France as he was a promise breaker and would betray the State..." The first letter written by Ammonio, his successor, says 'how the Signory's peace and league with France caused great displeasure to everyone in England.' (67)

If Carmelianus was known for his close links with the Venetians, then it may have been this tactical switch of

Venetian policy, settling their differences with the French, which led to his being replaced by someone else who might now be seen as more useful. Andrea Ammonio was younger, but of a similar background. Indeed it seems he first came to England, in 1506, in the company of Silvestro Gigli, nephew of Giovanni, who had been appointed Bishop of Worcester in succession to his uncle.

There is no point at which Carmelianus can be seen as helping the Venetians in any way that might have been detrimental to English interests. But did he benefit from his links with Venice and other foreign powers? There are no lack of offers of reward made in the correspondence. Much of this, however, was probably routine practice at the time. If the Venetians were making payments to Carmelianus, it was done discretely enough to leave no direct trace.

Whilst we cannot point to anything in Carmelianus' character suggesting that he would have turned down payments from the Venetians, the fact is that he was being well rewarded by the English king. Henry VII was himself "famous for the precision of his continental information, and this nearly all came from unofficial agents." (68) It is unlikely that the king would easily have been taken in by double-dealing in his own employ. It looks more likely that Carmelianus' cosy relations with Venice were well understood, and thought to be useful by the English court.

The one area in which he can be manifestly shown to have drawn on his credit with the Venetian State was in helping his own family back in Italy. A document of 1499, makes it clear that he has been influential in gaining a grant of full citizenship for his father and family in Brescia. (69)

A few years after he left the post of Latin Secretary, approaches are made on behalf of one of his nephews. (70) At the end of October 1516, the Venetian ambassador, writes to the Doge saying that Pietro Carmeliano, "heretofore secretary of the late most serene father of this King, has earnestly besought him, on behalf of his nephew, that he might be provided with 'some small employment in his native city of Brescia, or in its territory.' (71) There is an accompanying letter by Carmelianus himself, recalling his former service to the State, and in particular how he 'took very great pains, especially to mitigate and appease the wrath of the reigning Pope Julius II against your highness and your State.". This letter is written for the nephew himself to present to the Doge in person. (72)

This intervention was succesful. In September 1517 a decree is issued by the Council of Ten in Venice, "appointing Cyprian de Maialo, nephew of the Reverend Dom. Pietro Crameliano, Latin S of Heny VIII, captain of the *Devedo* of Rovigo for life." (73)

This is the last such evidence we have. Carmelianus is no longer in a position to offer useful service to Venice. He is now in his mid sixties, and has been away from his home country for some 40 years. His parents would no longer be alive, and perhaps not all his siblings. The ties must have begun to slacken.

CHURCHMAN AND ....

What happened to Peter Carmelianus once he lost his post as Latin Secretary to the king? His ecclesiastical appointments continued to grow in number over the years.

He was granted the prebend of the collegiate chapel of St Stephen, Westminster in January 1493. (73) In April 1501 he was presented to the canonry and prebend of Ampleforth in the cathedral church of York. (74) He also became Chaplain to the king.

In June 1504 another Papal document was issued, mentioning St George's. (76) He is now addressed as Archdeacon of Llandaff, his latest acquisition. Here Innocent VIII 'dispensed him to receive and retain for life together with the parish church, called a rectory, of St George, Sodwerke, in the suburbs of London....one other and without the said church any two other benefices, with cure or otherwise incompatible....' The document continues with technical qualifications, but the gist of it is that he may hold 'up to four other similar or dissimilar benefices...provided that of the four not more than two shall be parish churches...' Still this was not the end of his preferments. In 1511 he was made Archdeacon of Gloucester, resigning it in 1517 when he became prebendary of Ealdland in St Paul's.

At the same time though, he continued to maintain his presence at court, probably still acting as a royal chaplain, and sometimes called upon to write a diplomatic letter.

...MUSICIAN?

In 1512, the royal accounts contain the mention of a grant 'for Petrus of Brescia' of an annuity of £40. (77) Mention of the payment of this grant can be traced in the royal accounts for a number of subsequent years, and we can assume that it was an annual payment. (78) Something rather curious appears to be happening here. In 1513, Henry VIII mounted an invasion of France. The expedition was assembled with much ceremony and show, and lists survive of "the names of the retinue of the lords, knights and other noblemen now mustered." The list of the 'Myddlewarde' of the army begins with the "The King, with his horsemen," includes "the King's secretary of Latin" (Ammonio) and continues with all kinds of clerks and attendants, until we come to "Petre de Brescia, luter.". Various trumpeters, the King's 'minstrels and players' then follow. (79)

Is the sixty-two year old Carmelianus really going abroad with the army, in order to play the lute for His Majesty on campaign? There are other mentions of 'Peter the Luter' in the accounts of the royal household. (80) Most interesting is a letter of 1515, written by Nicolo Sagundino, who came to London that year as secretary to the Venetian ambassador.

He writes back, giving an account of their 'troublesome voyage' and their reception at court in Greenwich. "After dinner was a concert, where the writer was desired to play upon the clavichords and organ; among the audience was a Brescian to whom the King gives 300 ducats annually for playing the lute." He says that this person had expressed a desire to him "to have some new ballads sent him that he may please the King." (81)

Earlier commentators drew different conclusions as to whether or not this could be the same person. (82) The coincidence seems remarkable. The adopted name 'Carmelianus' is derived from the Latin word for a song, so he probably had musical abilities. Though it does sound an improbable career move, we should beware of judging another period by our own standards. Henry VIII had an active interest in music, playing, singing and composing himself, as well as encouraging the musical life of the court as a whole. He was very open to new influences from Europe.

In fact, closer study of the sources has shown that a second person must be involved. There is a record of a New Year's gift in 1528 – the year after the death of Carmelianus – made to 'Peter, luter, and his wife'. (83) The author of the revised entry on Carmelianus in the new edition of the Dictionary of National Biography suggests that this might have been a relative – perhaps another 'nephew' of the churchman. (84)

THE COMPANY OF SCHOLARS

Some insight into the character of Carmelianus can be gained from the correspondence of the great Dutch scholar Erasmus. Erasmus was famous throughout Western Europe as the foremost of humanist scholars in the next generation. He was in England on more than one occasion, and was familiar with a whole circle of leading humanists in this country. In 1506 he wrote an elegant and flattering little verse, dedicated to Peter Carmelianus, thanking him for a gift (85) Six years later, he is asking someone to convey thanks and good wishes to

Carmelianus "For to me it was undoubtedly both an honour and a pleasure to be praised by a man himself so greatly praised." (86)

One editor comments that "if we are to judge from [these two passages] Erasmus cared a great deal for the goodwill of Pietro Carmigliano" (87) And yet, an exchange of letters between Erasmus and Ammonio in 1513 shows a distinctly different attitude towards him.

That year, after the battle of Flodden in which the English forces, led by the Earl of Surrey, inflicted a devastating defeat on the Scots, Carmelianus published a celebratory poem. In it he rails against the Scottish king, James IV, who had died in the battle, along with many of his nobility and their troops.

Ammonio, who had just returned from accompanying the king on his expedition to France, writes to Erasmus in Cambridge, saying "Pietro Carmeliano has lately published an epitaph on the king of Scots which is full of womanish abuse". He says that Carmelianus is 'complacent and self-admiring' about it, "yet, if I had not pulled him up, he would have put in the word *pullulare* with the first syllable short! Still there is great deal for you to laugh at, especially the fact that people can be found to praise this sort of nonsense in all seriousness." Erasmus responds in kind, particularly relishing the mistake that Carmelianus had made in his versification. He asks Ammonio "...are you not being just a little too kind-hearted when you seek to defend that monster" and saying he would have given a great deal for him to have said nothing and allowed the error to be published.

A few days later he writes again, telling Ammonio that in defending his countryman (Carmelianus) "...you overlook his rascality!." He goes on, "I wish you could remove all the man's faults – if you did this you would do still better for your country's reputation - I mean remove the accursed creature entirely." (88)

These are the letters of two clever men, amusing each other by being bitchy about their contemporaries. Carmelianus is by no means the only person to be savaged. However, the poem celebrating the victory at Flodden certainly did not show him in his best light, and it may be significant that it was his last known attempt to write verse about major current events. The small error in his Latin scansion would have been embarrassing for him, had not Ammonio picked it up before it was put into circulation.

Erasmus, however, had a more particular reason for his hostile reaction to Carmelianus' poem about Flodden. A few years earlier, while he was in Italy, he had joined the household of Alexander Stuart. This young man, an illegitimate son of the Scottish king, James IV, had been appointed Archbishop of St Andrew's and had gone to Padua to study canon law. Erasmus taught him logic and rhetoric, and they visited Rome together. The scholar thought well of the young man's character and had good hopes for his future. However, Alexander had returned to Scotland and, despite his ecclesiastical status, had died on the battlefield of Flodden, along with his father. This loss, together with Erasmus' generally pacific outlook, would have given him good cause to feel distaste for a poem boasting about the victory.

The correspondence also reflects the competitive world in which they lived. Writers and academics readily view their peers as rivals, at the best of times. Both of the two correspondents are younger than Carmelianus, and they are on the way to supplanting him and his like. It was thirty years now since he had first won his place at court through writing poetry for public occasions. It may well be that they considered his style old-fashioned. He was also a well rewarded member of the establishment, maybe a little overblown in the person as well as on the page, and an obvious target for the jokes of his younger rivals.

There is one further letter that gives us a more favourable picture. Thomas More wrote to Erasmus in 1516, and talks of

Carmelianus: "He is entirely devoted to theology, and has performed the task of reading almost all the writers of fashionable disputation....We had a full dress discussion, each scratching the other's back with formal speeches and long panegyrics. Seriously, however, I like him thoroughly; he seems to me a man of real integrity, very learned, and now most devoted to research in the Scriptures. Lastly, but in my opinion by no means least, he has a high opinion of you." (89)

All this is a little confusing – 'rascality' in a 'man of real integrity'; a person full of faults, whose good opinion was greatly valued; an opportunist, profiting from church livings, who is now 'devoted to theology' and study of the Scriptures. More's description does give the impression of a learned man, if also rather long-winded and with out-dated mannerisms; a person whom it was possible both to respect, yet at the same time as take as a figure of fun. (90)

THE LAST YEARS

During the final dozen years of his life we catch fewer glimpses of Peter Carmelianus. What information there is relates mostly to his material circumstances. He paid a price for his financial well-being in 1522. King Henry raised a 'Forced Loan' on people of substance, in order to pay for a new war against France. The clergy were not exempt. "Mr Petrus Carmelianus was assessed for £331.6s.8d." (91) This was a considerable sum for one individual, and indicates how substantial his means were thought to be.

From the final years there is evidence of activities that were more commercial than ecclesiastical. In October 1526 a licence was granted to import wine and wood from France. This is in the name of 'Peter de Brisia' – who may perhaps be indentified with the 'Peter the Luter' who was still receiving gifts from the king a year after the death of Carmelianus. (92) Two years earlier there is a record of involvement in a complicated property deal, concerning land and tenements 'at Kingston-upon-Thames'. Here the person involved was 'Peter

Carmelian, archdeacon of Gloucester and prebendary of St Stephen's, Westminster'. Perhaps he was having to re-order his financial affairs after they had been raided by the king? (93)

The exact date of his death is not certain, but his successor to the benefice of St George's, Southwark, a man called William Middleton, another lawyer, took up office before the end of 1527.

There is one interesting postscript to Carmelianus's life, in a letter from the Bishop of Chichester to Cardinal Wolsey in April 1529. By this time, the campaign for the annullment of the King's first marriage, to Catherine of Aragon, was in full flow. Documents were being gathered, and among the most pertinent would be those relating to the dispensation which Pope Julius II had granted, twenty years before, allowing Henry to marry the wife of his deceased brother.

The Bishop of Chichester writes: "Peter Carmelianus was in his time the keeper of the King's original letters, and was accustomed to keep all the replies of the Pope, and of others writing in Latin." (94) The original negotiations happened when Carmelianus was Latin Secretary to the King's father, and he would probably have drafted the correspondence with Rome. Now the paperwork was urgently needed. If it had gone astray, Carmelianus would be a convenient person to blame, since he had recently died and was safely out of reach of King Henry's displeasure.

THE BRINK OF CHANGE

The catalogue of early Rectors of the parish progresses from the briefest glimpses of figures who are little more than names, through to men who played a significant part on the national stage and about whose careers, and even characters, a good deal of information can be gathered. After this point the national church undergoes radical change, with the break from Rome, and the introduction of sweeping reforms.

The list of Rectors of the parish would go on, with a continuing mix of the obscure and the distinguished. In the 17th and 18th centuries there would be an eminent mathematician and astronomer, as well as others who were also literary men or lecturers, who published writings, not only on theology, but also politics, or who were chaplains to members of the aristocracy. All of them would have had a staff of assistant clergy to carry out the day to day ministry in the parish. From Elizabethan times onward, the Rector, together with the Churchwardens and the Overseers of the Poor, began to acquire new responsibilities as parishes were called upon to provide the 'social services' previously provided by monastic houses. The Vestry developed into the local authority for the parish area and, by the 19th century, the huge expansion of population would have made chairing the Vestry meeting a very demanding task in itself. The Rector was only relieved of this responsibility with the creation of the new metropolitan boroughs at the beginning of the 20th century.

It is not easy to assess men like Gigli or Carmelianus, in their role as Rector of St George's, Southwark. The evidence does not give us much to say. It is most unlikely that, with all their other commitments, either spent much time in the parish. However, that would not then have been unusual. Other Rectors will have held the living in plurality, and paid clergy to carry out their duties for them. The real issue would be how much care and attention they gave to overseeing the delegation of such responsibilities. If they took trouble to appoint good priests, and kept a check on the life and welfare of the parish, it could still have benefited. If this sort of care was lacking, then having a courtier as Rector might have been detrimental.

What we do know is that the Guild of St George was at its most active during the period of their incumbencies. Three priests were supported, and papal permission was given for a fund-raising drive in support of their work. New studies, still continuing, seem to suggest that some major building project was under way at the church, during the second half of Carmelianus' time. Opposite the church stood the palace of one of the most influential men in the kingdom – a palace that was soon to pass into royal hands. It was also during the years of Carmelianus' incumbency that the Breviary of Therouanne was given to the church.

It does seem possible to suggest that the early Tudor period may well have been a good time in the history of St George's. It appears to have been a church that was able to attract donations, it had some of the most influential people in the land coming and going in the neighbourhood, and it did have the patronage of wealthy Rectors, with very good connections. Even if they only made rare appearances at the church themselves, it may well be that they presided over a period when the parish basked in a small corner of sunshine, before the upheavals of the Reformation, were to begin.

NOTES ON 'THE EARLY CLERGY'

1. M. Carlin, p.289f.
2. PRO. E40/6112
3. Marjorie Chibnall, "Monks and Pastoral Work: a problem in Anglo-Norman history", *Journal of Ecclesiastical History Vol 18 (1967)* p.141.
4. B.R. Kemp, "Monastic Possession of Parish Churches in England in the Twelfth Century" *Journal of Ecclesiastical History Vol 31, No.2* pp.144/4, n.50. See also R. Fletcher, *The Conversion of Europe*, Harper Collins 1997, p.482.
5. "Chartulary of the Hospital of St Thomas the Martyr, Southwark (1213 – 1525)" Published privately for the Governors of St Thomas Hospital 1932. p.63
6. Reg. Woodlock , ed. A.W. Goodman, 9th Sept. 1307
7. C.J. Offer, *The Bishop's Register*, Addit. Note B, p.226, quoting from E.H. Pearce.
8. When the present writer became Rector of St George's in 1991, he found the parish in financial difficulties and seriously in arrears with its payments to the Diocese. During the next two or three years, until the position was stabilised, it was a regular occurrence for the Archdeacon to telephone at the beginning of the month, asking the rector when the next payment could be expected. The continuities of church life are many and various!
9. Reg. Woodlock, ed. A.W. Goodman, 2nd Feb. 1309 (p.337)
10. Manning & Bray, "The History and Antiquities of the County of Surrey", 1814, vol.iii, p.636
11. Chartulary of St Thomas' Hospital, no. 294
12 Reg. Edington, ed. Dom S.F. Hockey, Vol 2, 323:259., & Vol 1, 236:1540.
13. "Exchange was a practice which first became noteworthy in the 13th century and reached a climax verging on scandal toward the end of the 14th." (Peter Heath, *The English Parish Clergy on the Eve of the Reformation,* London 1969.)
14. There is, however, a record, preserved in the Chartulary of St Thomas Hospital (no. 593), of a grant by 'John Pelham and Thomas Mottyng, clerk, to Nicholas Carren and Henry Baylyf of Southwerk, of all lands and tenements they bought of Stephen Skarlet, in the parish of Lambeth.' This is dated 1384, some 15 years after the death of Thomas, though the coincidence of another 'clerk' of the same name in the same area is interesting.
15. Reg. Wykeham, ed. Thomas F. Kirby, vol. 11, p.27.

16. Sudbury Register, 8th June 1370 (from Virginia Davis, "Clergy in London in the Late Middle Ages", IHR 2000.)
17. May McKisack, "The Fourteenth Century", Oxford 1959, p. 226
18. *Cal. Pat. Rolls 1367-70, p. 317; BRUO.*
19. See Virginia Davis, op.cit..
20. Reg. Wykeham, ed. Kirby II, fol. 170 r
21. Reg. Wykeham's Reg. ed. Kirby, Vol 13, p.431
22. Reg. Beaufort, fol. 27 r.
23. Brooke does not appear in the early lists, such as that of Manning & Bray. Martha Carlin gives a reference to the *Calendar of Patent Rolls 1422-9.* However, I have not been able to trace this record. The corresponding section of the actual Roll does not seem to relate to St George's or to William Brooke. The index to the Rolls Series volume does list a Dom. William Brooke, but he is 'rector of the church of St Michael, Paternoster-cherche, in the Riole, London' in 1425, and continues there in 1432.
24. Peter Heath, *op.cit.* p.56f
25. *Reg, Waynflete, i, fol.35r* and B.R.U.O.
26. B.R.U.O. lists some 20 different church appointments held by Hooper between his ordination in 1423 and his death by 1454.
27. Robert C. Palmer, *Selling the Church. The English Parish in Law, Commerce and Religion 1350-1550.* North Carolina 2002, p.11
28. *ibid.* p.87
29. Reg.Waynflete, I, fol. 35r. Such exchanges of livings had become quite common by the late fourteenth century. A study of the *acta* of Bishop Courtenay of London, 1375-81, shows this to be the largest group of such transcations: "...they are of two kinds: commissions to other bishops to effect exchanges, and certificates of execution..." (A.K. McHardy, *The Church in London 1375-1392,* London Record Society, 1977.) Waynflete's registers have not been transcribed or translated, and I have to admit that I have not gone through every word of this lengthy text. Most of it, however, does appear to be the usual bureaucratic formulas.
30. Reg.Waynflete, I, fol 50 v.
31. B.R.U.O. & Reg. Wayneflete II, fol 2 v, and 3 v.
32. Reg. Wayneflete II, 89 v.
33. B.R.U.O.
34. BRUO – Gigli

35. The Register does, however, describe 'John Gylis' as Papal Subdeacon and Collector, helping to confirm the identity. (Reg. Wayneflete vol. ii, f.47)

36. *48th Annual Report of the Deputy Keeper of the Public Records*, London 1887, p.387

37. *Cal. Pat. Rolls*. 1476-85 p.74

38. D. Hay, "Pietro Griffo, An Italian in England 1506-1512" *Italian Studies* Vol II 1939, pp.118-128

39. B.L. MS Vitel. B II ff.144 et.seq. – quoted by Hay

40. Hay, op.cit. p.123

41. D. Wilkins, *Concilia Magnae Britanniae et Hiberniae*, iii, 613

42. B. L.. Harley MS 336

43. Maecenas was a wealthy Roman, in the time of Augustus, who was a patron of the poets Virgil and Horace, among others. His name became a byword for wealthy benefactors of the arts.

44. *Materials Henry VII*, i, 198

45. Curt F. Bühler, "Three Letters from Henry VII to the Dukes of Milan", *Speculum 31*, 1956, pp. 485-90

46. The traditional lists of Rectors give 1510 as a starting date for Carmelianus. This is because there is another gap in the Bishop's Registers, and he first appears there at that date. However, there are other available sources, both from papal registers and ordination records from London diocese, which confirm his earlier appointment. Information on his Brescian background was assembled by Paolo Guerrini, "Pietro Carmiliano da Brescia", editrice *'Brixia Sacra'* 1918.

47. *Materials Henry VII* Vol II p.244 and p.289.

48. Reg.. Kempe f. 226v & 227r. See Virginia Davis, 'Clergy in London in the later Middle Ages'. London 2000.

49. Reg. Hill f. 2r. . See Virginia Davis, ibid. The details of Carmeliano's ordination and appointment to St George's seem to have escaped many of those who have compiled information about him. Neither Gardiner (DNB) nor Emden (BRUO) list is appointment to St George's. Manning & Bray give the date of his appointment to the parish as 1510 – an error which has been literally engraved in stone on the list of Rectors in the church itself. His ordination took place in London, at St Paul's, on letters dimissory from the Bishop of Winchester. There are no extant ordination lists for the time of Bishop Kempe. Carmelianus was made sub-deacon and deacon during vacancy of the see, the ordinations being conducted by a suffragan, James Wall, Bishop of Kildare. By the date of his priesting, however, Bishop Hill was in post.

50 *Cal. Papal Reg.* Innocent VIII, no. 375.

51. Pluralism would be one of the issues of concern to the Reformers, but they too failed to resolve the matter. A Pluralities Act was passed in 1838, forbidding clergy in the Church of England from holding more than one benefice at a time, except by dispensation of the Archbishop of Canterbury.

52. M. Carlin, p.64.

53. Later the house became a Royal Mint, and then was granted to the Archbishop of York, who sold it in 1557. After this it began to be broken up.

54. See separate article on the *Guild of St George.* That St George's had some place in the thoughts of Henry VII, even if only a topographical one, is suggested by the provision in his Will of "2000 L. to be spent on repair of highways and bridges from Windsor to Richmond manor and thence to St George's Church, beside Southwark, and thence to Greenwich manor and thence to Canterbury." His funeral procession came from Richmond to 'St George's in the Fields', where it was met by clergy, before proceeding to London Bridge and St Paul's.

55. Bernard André may well have come over to England with Henry when he came to claim the throne.

56. A full account of this literary exchange, together with text and prose translation of the poems of both Gaguin and Carmelianus, is given by Donald Carlson in an article "Politicizing Tudor Court Literature: Gaguin's Embassy and Henry VII's Humanists' Response", in *Studies in Philology* Vol. LXXXV, 3. 1988 pp. 279-304. The translation of Carmelianus' reply to Robert Gaguin given here is by the author.

57. Carlson does make the point that there was actually no personal animosity involved in this exchange. In 1498 Robert Gaguin published a volume which included some lines he had written in praise of Carmelianus, and which appears to be in reciprocation for some flattery which has passed the other way. This cosmopolitan group of humanist scholars may well have felt more in common with each other than they did with the courts they served and for whom they wrote.

58. *D.N.B.*

59. from a manuscript notebook deposited at the Warburg Institute (NAM 25).

60. Bühler, commenting on two letters written by Carmelianus, now surviving in an American library, says "These will be of particular interest to students of calligraphy, for they are fine

examples of writing from the pen of the man who brought the Italian hand to England." *Speculum 31*

61. *Cal. Letters Spain* Vol. Henry VII. no. 99. . The Latin text of a letter by Carmelianus to Ferdinand & Isabella is given in *Letters & Papers illustrative of the reigns of Richard III & Henry VII,* ed. J. Gardiner, pp. 100-2.

62 *Cal. Papers Venice* Vol I no.771

63. ibid. no. 776.

64. ibid. no.918

65. D. Carlson, "English Humanist Books", University of Toronto, 1993, Ch 2, p.195, n.i

66. *Letters and Papers Henry VIII,* 1509: 20

67. *Cal. Papers Venice* Vol II nos. 251 & 254.

68. J.R. Hale, 'International Relations in the West' *NCMH,* p.268.

69. P. Guerrini, "Pietro Carmeliano da Brescia", p.10 f.68.

70. Pietro appears to have been one of several children in his family, and doubtless would have had nephews and nieces. However, we should perhaps not entirely overlook the fact that this was a period in which to speak of the 'nephew' of church dignitary was sometimes taken as synonymous with referring to illegitimate offspring.

71. *Cal. Papers Venice* Vol.3, no.1488

72. ibid. no. 1489. Carmelianus here reminds the Doge especially of the part he played in the crisis of 1510.

73. *Cal. Papers Venice* Vol.2 no.963

74. *Cal. Pat. Rolls* Vol. I 30th Jan 1493. This had become vacant through the resignation of Master Oliver King, the king's secretary.

75. ibid. Vol II 14th April 1501

76. *Cal. Papal Reg.*, Vol XV, no. 383.

77. *Letters & Papers of Henry VIII,* Vol I, no. 3473, 'given at Greenwich on 13 October in the fourth year of Henry VIII'.

78. ibid. Vol II, nos, 1168 & 2736, Vol III, no. 999.

79. *Letters & Papers Henry VIII*, no. 4314.

80. ibid. Vol IV. no. 348.

81. ibid. Vol II 3rd May 1515, N. Sagundino to A. Foscari.

82. Gardiner in *D.N.B.* identifies Peter the Luter as Carmelianus, whereas Emden directly contradicts this saying he is 'to be distinguished from Peter de Brescia....a lute-player in the kings retinue in the middle ward of his army in France, 1513."

83. Letters & Papers HenryVIII, 3748

84. J.B. Trapp. He also draws attention to an Alice Carmillan/Ellis Carmyllyan, painter and milliner, who worked on the elaborate decoration of Greenwich Palace in 1527, along with several Italian artists and Hans Holbein.

85. See Dr C. Reedijk, *The Poems of Desiderius Erasmus,* no.

86. "The Correspondence of Erasmus", trans. R.A.B. Mynors & D.F.S. Thomson, University of Toronto, 1975, Letter 262, to Andrea Ammonio,

87. Reedijk, p.70

88. ibid. Letters 280, 282, & 283,

89. ibid. Letter 461.

90. Would the 'writers of fashionable disputation' have included Martin Luther or other early reformers? Five years later Henry VIII used the near contemporary scholar John Fisher and others to help prepare the treatise on the *Seven Sacraments*, which was to earn the king the title 'Defender of the Faith' from Pope Leo X. Maybe Carmelianus also had some role as a theological consultant to the king?

91. *Letters & Papers Henry VIII*, Vol III, 2483.

92. ibid. Vol IV no. 2599

93. ibid. Vol IV, no. 348

94. ibid. Vol IV, no. 5465.

AN AMENDED LIST OF EARLY RECTORS

(around 1144/50	Robertus, priest)
(1241 >	Ralph de Dunion ?)
< 1245 >	Martin
1307 - 1315	William de Alyngio
1315 >	Alard de Alyngio
1317/18 >	William de Halybourn
1349 - 1362	Everard de Pratellis *alias* Volet
1362 - 1369	Thomas Mottyng
1370 – post 1406	Thomas Profete
< 1428 >	William Brooke ?
< 1450	Robert Amyas
1450 - 1451	William Hooper
1451 - 1452	Rowland Banes
1452 >	Roger Potter *alias* Redonall
< 1470	Thomas Candour
1470	William Moggys
1470 - 1477	John Fox
1477 - 1482	Giovanni Gigli ('John Gylis')
1482 - 1489	John Brown
1490 - 1527	Peter Carmelianus

THE HASTINGS STONES

The oldest objects in St George's Church are also the most inaccessible and the least well known. They remain unseen by most of the congregation and visitors.

High up in the tower, above the ringing chamber, above the belfry itself where the great bells – re-cast before the present church was built - hang in the gloom, up in the chamber which houses the mechanism of the clock, two inscribed stones have been set into the wall. They are deeply carved with a Gothic script, not easily read now, even by the practised eye. But the text on one of them makes it clear that these stones are 300 years older than the stonework into which they are set.

Along with two brass memorial plaques and the pipework of the organ, they seem to have been salvaged from the demolition of the previous building. But why have they been set in such an obscure location? A short article about these stones, which appeared in an antiquarian journal shortly after the Second World War, describes them as having been `recently discovered'. This sounds a little odd, as they had never been lost, and would always have been familiar to the handful of people who had occasion to go into that remote room. However, it indicates that they were unknown to the wider world, and even to those whose field of study gave them a particular interest in what they have to say. (1)

THE LAW-SUIT

One of the stones is a little larger than the other. It measures 24 x 22 inches, and the text on it reads as follows:

Edwardus
dñs de Haſting/hastys
me dni/fieri fecit
anno dñi mil

e*f*imo CCCC
XXX VIII

"Edward, lord of Hastings, had me made in the year of our Lord 1437"

They have been identified readily enough with a person of that name, known to have died at that date, and who had a significant link with the parish. Edward Hastings was one of the parties to a well-documented law-suit, at the beginning of the fifteenth century, which is still of significance in the study of heraldry,.

He was the second son of Sir Hugh Hastings, whose lands were mostly in Norfolk and who had served on several campaigns during the reign of Richard II. The elder son, also called Hugh, succeeded but died without issue. Edward was just 14 years old when his brother died in 1495.

The lawsuit stemmed from the death of the Earl of Pembroke, in December 1389, to whom they were related. One of his titles was *Lord Hastings*. Hugh, Edward's older brother, had been declared heir to the title in 1389, after the death of a cousin, but, at this point, their right to the title was disputed by Reynold, Lord Grey of Ruthin, who claimed a stronger right to the title, and whatever inheritance went with it. The Hastings claim to the title was in the male line, but through a cousin `of the ***half-blood'***, while Lord Grey's claim was through the female line, but from a sister `of the ***full-blood'***.

The whole case is couched in the terminology of heraldry and pedigree. The issue that was the subject of the law case was the right to bear 'the undifferenced arms of Hastings', as if it were all to do with names and style, rather than matters of property and power. The arms in question are described as ***'or, a maunche gules'*** , and Edward's father had carried the Hastings arms on his various military campaigns.

Edward succeeded his brother in 1396. In 1399 he was knighted by the King, who also granted him £40 a year to help maintain his estate during his minority. The case was moved against him by Lord Grey in the first year of the new century, and in the Second Parliament of Henry IV he petitioned that a curator should be appointed for his opponent, who was still under age, to help move things forward. The case, however, made slow progress. It was not finally heard in the Court of Chivalry until 1410. Judgement was handed down on 9th May, in favour of Lord Grey, and very heavy costs were awarded against Hastings.

The outcome cannot have been a total surprise. In 55 out of the 79 inquisitions that were taken after the Earl of Pembroke died, Lord Grey was found to be the heir. At the Coronation of Henry IV, in the same year that the suit was begun, Grey had claimed the right to carry out certain ceremonial duties attached to the title – 'to carry the Great Spurs and the Second Sword, and to perform the office of Napperer'. His claim was allowed. Hastings was to claim the same duties at the coronation of Henry V in 1413, but his claim was not allowed.

In 1400 there was not just a new reign, but a change of dynasty, as Richard II was deposed in favour of the Lancastrian, Henry Bolinbroke. Grey, being that much older, would have had better opportunity to forward himself, and win favour with the new establishment. He was summoned to Parliament in 1389, where he was among those who both gave assent to the secret imprisonment of Richard, and passed the Acts of Succession for Henry IV. (2) Although Hastings' father had Lancastrain connections, having served with John of Gaunt, the young man had got himself into enough trouble to be committed to the Tower in 1403, and had to surrender rights in a property to the King in order to get himself out.

The judgement and award of costs against him in 1410 was a heavy blow, which would probably have relegated him to a place among the lesser gentry, with little influence or prestige. He appealed against the judgement, and refused to pay the costs awarded, lest in paying them he should seem to concede the justice of the case against him.

After the accession of Henry V several commissions were issued for hearing the appeal, but larger affairs of state kept preventing the necessary people from being brought together. In 1417 the appeal was again resumed, but before it could come to anything, Lord Grey had Hastings arrested for non-payment of the earlier costs. He was charged in the sum of £987, and confined in the Marshalsea prison. He was to spend most of the rest of his life there.

THE PRISONER

Whether he ever set foot in St George's Church is unknown, but he was a forced resident in its parish. Perhaps he could see the church from his window or, more likely perhaps, one of the clergy from St George's came to minister to him in his confinement.

A small group of letters, written by Edward Hastings from prison, have survived. They give the sharpest insight we have into the state of mind of this unhappy man. One of them, addressed to Grey, begins:

"Sir Reynald Grey lord of Rethyn be thenkith yowe howe ye have kept me Edward Lord Hastynges in prison ny thre yere and an half thurgh which distresse in prison my body and my lemys ar aperted and I brought in til langweryn sickenesse that I am nevir like to be heile. But evir more to endure in febilnesse til god departe my soule fro my body And also in the long distresse of prisonement my wife is dede my childryn and my servauntz that be goddis grace myght have levid and fard wel ne had my desese and duresse of prison be, and ther to me wordly levyng is be nome me as hit may be for the time I thanke god of my febilnesse and my povert And therefore on goddis be halve be thenkith yowe whate joye is in hevyn and what payne is in helle and whethir ye holde me in prison by lordship mayntenaunce richesse or power or by gode concience lawe right or reson And therfor I pray yowe sende me substancial worde what and howe ye wil...ordeyne pfer to me touchyng myn armes and myn enheritaunce which of right is discendid unto me aftir the desese of Sir John Hastyngs Erle of Penbroke and wher to I shal triste and whethir ye will lete me dye in prison or none or what remedye yowe liketh to ordeyne for my duresse in prison For my time is shorte of life I suppose and to dye in prison I am like so as I ly bounden in feteris of iryn in the Marschy....." (3)

Some attempts were made to settle the dispute. We find Hastings proposing, from prison, that his son, John, should marry one of Lord Grey's daughters, and the rights be passed on to them, and that he should be released without any payment of costs as part of this settlement. Even in this proposal though, he is wanting to insist that he can prove that the rights of inheritance are his to pass on. His opponent, on the other hand, seems to have been insisting on some sort of payment, as a recognition of the justice of his claim. It is not surprising that the negotiations broke down, leaving Edward "...to be fettered and kept in duresse of prison where that men for tres[on], felons, and condempned men, goñ at large...."

Even as he is writing to Grey about possible terms of an agreement, he is also calling down a curse on any of his heirs who fail to defend the claim for which he has been imprisoned: "...whiche decent ryght cleyme and inherytaunce Godes curse and myn have all myn eyres that wyll not sue the ryght aftyr me..." Notwithstanding such words, his son never prosecuted the claim and subsequent heirs seem to have quietly let the matter drop. (4)

THE SECOND STONE

Nothing is known of the final three years of Hastings' life, between the time when the last of the letters were written, and his death in 1437. It is possible that he was eventually released from prison. However, the second of the two stones in the tower of St George's might suggest otherwise. 16 x 22 inches in size, it reads:

Hec requies mea
in sclm scli hic ha
bitabo qm elegi

The Survey of London, rather unhelpfully, offers only an anachronistic paraphrase in the words of Romeo – 'O! here will a set my everlasting rest'. F.A. Greenhill, in his note of 1953, offers both an expansion of the Latin abbrevations –

'Hec requies mea/in s(e)c(u)l(u)m s(e)c(u)li hic ha/bitabo q(uonia)m elegi(m)' –

and also a serviceable translation: "This is my repose to all eternity; here will I take up my habitation, since I have chosen it."

What both seem to have missed is that the text is surely an adapted quotation from the Bible. Psalm 132 v.15, in the *Book of Common Prayer,* is translated "This shall be my rest for ever: here will I dwell, for I have a delight therein." If we take the text from the Vulgate, the Latin Bible of the Middle Ages (5), and set that alongside the text of the inscription, the parallel can be clearly enough seen:

Vulgate: haec est requies mea in sempiternum his habitabo quia desideravi eam
Inscription: hec requies mea in sclm scli hic habitabo qm elegi ea

The substitution of *seculum seculi* for *sempiternum* is straightforward, especially if the text was being cited from memory. The end of the text must have been adapted to suit the circumstance. There was no `delight' involved for Hastings, but there is the acknowledgement that his resting place is one he has chosen – through his obduracy in refusing to settle the legal costs awarded against him, lest this should also seem to concede his case.

This particular verse was part of the rite used when an anchorite was closed up in a cell, entering into voluntary confinement for a life of prayer. (6) An educated man of the time would quite likely have been aware of this. If Hastings himself chose the words for his epitaph, it may indicate something of his state of mind. It suggests the attempt at some sort of religious accommodation to his circumstances, at least toward the end of his life. Did he come to see his prison cell, alongside of St George's, as a kind of anchorage, to which he was finally reconciled? If so, being buried in a tomb close by would be a symbolic continuation of his enforced status as an anchorite of the parish.

The last of the letters does suggest a certain resignation, where he speaks of himself as "...trew prisoner tyll the tyme that God take hym by fayre deth in to hys grace so that he be noth myscheved ne maymed in armes now in hys age...."

SURVIVAL

There remains the question of why these sad relics of a life sacrificed to family pride should be preserved now in such an obscure location? They are probably survivals of a tomb or chantry chapel within, or attached to, the medieval church. The report on the recent archaeology indicates evidence of chapel on the south side of the building, which appears to have had one major tomb in it – though nothing can yet be proved. (7)

Given the date, this is likely to have been built and ornamented in a Gothic style, matching the script on the stones. On stylistic grounds alone, they may have been regarded as out of place in a new Neo-Classical building of the 18th century. In addition, being Latin inscriptions and associated with the saying of Masses for the dead, they may have been regarded as too Roman in character to be suitable for public display. The new church was built within 20 years of the Hanoverian succession, and only a decade before the Jacobite rebellion of 1745. It's character exemplifies a strongly Protestant phase of the Anglican tradition.

There could then have been grounds, both of doctrine and of taste, that weighed against the inclusion of these stones in the fabric of the new building. Lodging them in the remotest part of the tower suggests that whoever wished to conserve them for their historical/antiquarian interest had a struggle to make their case. Either this was the best compromise they could reach, or it may even suggest a degree of subterfuge, smuggling them into the building, in a place where they would hardly ever be seen. Ironically, this obscure location may well have made for their better preservation.

NOTES

1. F.A. Greenhill, 'St George's, Southwark', in *Transactions of the Monumental Brass Society* Vol IX, part III, No. LXXIII (Autumn 1953) p.132.
2. Lord Grey did not have an entirely easy time, himself. In 1402, having been appointed by Henry, prince of Wales, as one of his Lieutenants in North Wales, he was taken prisoner by Owain Glyndwr. The Welsh leader demanded a ransom of 10,000 marks – 6,000 to be paid by the Feast of St Martin, on pain of death – and Grey's eldest son to be given as a hostage.
3 The surviving papers relating to the case were gathered together by C.G. Young, in a private publication of 1841 'An Account of the Controversy between Reginald Lord Grey of Ruthyn and Sir Edward Hastings....'
4. Within little more than a century, in fact, the male line of both families had failed, and the barony was in abeyance from 1542. It was eventually revived in the 19th century when, ironically perhaps, it was granted to a distant descendant of Hastings. C.G. Young's collection of the relevant documents was made in connection with this revival of the title.
5. Where it appears as Psalm 131:14
6. See Fiona Maddocks, *Hildegard of Bingen,* London 2001, pp. 28/9.
7. MoLAS 2007, *op.cit.* p.19

THE GUILD OF OUR LADY AND ST GEORGE

At the end of the Victorian era, when the Rector of St George's delivered his Annual Report, the list of parish activities and societies included:
Sunday Schools, Sunday Night Schools, Bible Classes, Band of Hope, a Girls' Club and ***a Club for Lads, Mothers' Meeting, Ladies Working Party, District Visiting, Football Club, Swimming Club, Chess Club, Parents' Social Gathering,*** as well as the Choir and arrangements for worship in several buildings. (1)

During the twentieth century, the range of parish activities narrowed at St George's, as in most places. Some of the educational, health and welfare provision, pioneered by churches in the 19th century, was been taken over by national government or local authorities. Many of the social activities declined in face of alternative leisure pursuits. Parishes today tend to be much less ambitious in the range of activities they promote, and their resources – especially in staffing – are certain to be less.

But what was the pattern in the Middle Ages? What went on at parish churches, apart from worship, before the time of the Reformation?

There is ample evidence to show that, as the main public building in an area, a parish church was used for a wider range of activities than is usual today. Any kind of public meeting might take place there, and other social and community gatherings as well. The origins of much medical and nursing care began with the churches, and in Southwark, in 1400, we find a reference to "the old aisle where the sick and poor lie within the church of the hospital of St Thomas the Martyr". Legal proceedings sometimes took place in churches. A man called John Rogers was tried in St Mary Overy in 1555, during the reign of Mary Tudor. (2)

At St George's we see this continue into a later period – as with the macabre occasion in 1610, when the register records the fate "Michael Banks out of the Kings Bench, executed: did revive again, was in the old vestry three hours and was then carried back to be executed again." On a more cheerful note, in Hogarth's picture of *Southwark Fair* in 1733, we can see the church in the background, very much a part of the scene, with plays and performances happening outside, with platforms and scenery apparently erected against the fabric of the old building itself.

However, the principal evidence of regular organised activities, during the medieval period, lies in the existence of parish Guilds or Fraternities. These were formally constituted bodies, often authorised by letters patent of the king, and were permitted to raise money in a number of ways for the discharge of their various objects. In this parish there existed a Fraternity of Our Lady and St George, from at least the mid fifteenth century, and probably earlier.

OBJECTS

What were the objects of the Guild? We do not have a documented list of the full activities of the guild at St George's. However, in the next door parish of St Margaret – whose church stood on the triangular site in Borough High Street where the War Memorial is now to be found – they had two Guilds. One of these was dedicated to St Katharine, and the other to the Assumption of the Blessed Virgin Mary. We are told that,

"The wardens kept the church, its fittings and vestments, in repair and paid the Clerk's wages and all the incidental expenses of the church services and festivals. The accounts show that the great festivals were celebrated with the traditional ceremonies, and there was a yearly procession with choir and banners to St Mary Overy Priory, but the high spot of the year was St Margaret's Day, when the church was specially decorated, extra 'singing men and boys' were engaged, and a large bonfire was lit at night. In the early accounts there are references to plays in the church...." (3)

The Fraternity of the Assumption at St Margaret's was established during the reign of Henry VI. William Rendle, however, draws attention to the records of an earlier Guild of St George, surviving from the previous century, at [Kings] Lynn. These date from 1376.

"The rules of this gild of St George at Linn were: - A priest to serve the altar of St George; to find candles and torches for service and burials; services for the dead and offerings; masses for souls; help to poor brethren and sisteren; four meetings every year under penalty; the gild to go to church, from their gild house, in hood and livery; every feast to be begun with prayer, the gild light burning the while, and always without noise and jangling; members admitted at general morun-speche (general mornspeech, or meeting); the affairs of the gild not to be disclosed." (4)

Rendle is very ready to link the date of the Southwark Guild of St George to the one documented at Kings Lynn: "Probably our St George's Gild, noted as it had now become, was of as early foundation". However, in 1389, during the reign of King Richard II, Parish Guilds were required to submit returns to the king. Against the background of unrest, inflamed by the Black Death, and culminating in the Peasants' Revolt, the government would have been wary of associations that might have been used as a cover for agitation or conspirators. Wardens and masters of all guilds were required to submit details of their foundation and form of government, describe their activities and list their property. (5)

These returns, of which 471 survive in the Public Record Office, provide a valuable snapshot of the pattern of parish guilds at that time. Among the returns, there are seven for different Guilds of St George around the country, but none for St George's at Southwarke. However, the returns that survive cover only part of the country – principally East Anglia, Lincolnshire and London. There are none at all for Surrey or Southwark, so they offer no conclusive evidence of whether a Southwark Fraternity existed at that stage, or not.

What the returns do give us is a fuller picture of the kind of activities undertaken by parish Guilds in the later Middle Ages. The purposes of the Guild at St George's in Southwark would have fitted within the wider pattern. There was usually a combination of religious and charitable objects – though they would not have made that distinction in the way we would today. One commentator writes , "At the heart of them lay delight in social activities: friends who lived near together or who had some common interest met regularly and celebrated at an annual feast, and it was social cohesion of the group which gave the fraternities their strength. In the medieval world such activities took place in a religious context." (6)

Prayer for the dead was also a significant part of their concern. "Most of the parish fraternities of the later Middle Ages provided for at least an annual requiem for dead brethren. This was an inestimable advantage for those of modest means who, unlike wealthy men and women, could not afford the considerable sums necessary for the endowment of a personal chantry priest or for an annual mass to be said in perpetuity." (7)

Saying prayers for the dead may sound, to modern ears, a strange object for a charity. We should remember though, that in the nineteenth century many Friendly Societies had their origin in groups of neighbours clubbing together to make sure that members' families could be given a decent funeral. Seeing that proper respect was paid to the dead has been both a social and religious obligation for communities all through the ages. The century or two before the Reformation was a time when most people in Europe saw that obligation as reaching beyond the point of burial, into a concern for their loved one's progress through Purgatory as well.

CHAPLAINS

We do know that the funds at St George's were used, at least in part, to maintain clergy. For a time the Fraternity was maintaining three priests at St George's, and there was usually at least one. At St Botolph without Aldersgate the duties of the fraternity's priest included saying annual and weekly masses and 'the daily early-morning mass for workmen.' After the annual requiem the names of all living and dead members of the fraternity were read. "Apart from his duties on behalf of the fraternity, the priest was obliged to assist the parish clergy." His salary for this was 10½ marks per annum. (8)

Sometimes the guild priest could function as an additional curate in the parish. However, a post with limited duties attached to it and no cure of souls, could, especially if it were in the big city, attract the less scrupulous members of the clergy. Chaucer, in the ***Canterbury Tales***, praises his Parson for having remained faithful as a village priest, and commends him that,

> He sette nat his benefice to hyre
> And leet his sheep encombred in the myre
> And ran to Londoun unto Seinte Poules
> To seken hym a chaunterie for soules,
> Or with a bretherhed to been witholde; (9)

Clergy deserting rural parishes to go to London, where they would try to find themselves a chaplaincy, was a serious problem in the 14th century. In 1362, Archbishop Simon Islip fixed the stipend of chaplains at a lower rate than that of parish priests, as a deliberate disincentive, and that differential was maintained. Half a century earlier his predecessor, Robert de Winchelsey, had ordered the attendance of chaplains at matins, vespers and other offices in the church. He also required them, "to swear, if called upon, to do no damage to the churches or chapels, to rectors or vicars, in the matter of perquisites, oblations and so forth, and also not to raise hatred, scandals or contentions between rectors and parishioners." (10) Clearly, this additional staffing was not always an unmixed blessing.

As the population of the parish increased there could well have been occupation enough for a guild chaplain at St George's, even in respect of the departed alone. William Rendle, however, is keen to enliven the proceedings further:
"This is the way they managed it: On the great festival of St George, there was a sort of jubilant procession of the Guilds of St George and St Margaret, not necessarily, but probably, to St George's, in Southwark, which from its position opposite a Royal palace, and from the high status of its patrons, was probably one of the best churches in the neighbourhood. The warrior saint was personated by a man on horseback, in glittering armour, bearing the banner of St George, a red cross on a white ground – the horse being arrayed in velvet. By his side a guild sister, arrayed as St Margaret; and between them was led, by a silken halter, a man dressed to imitate the scaly dragon vanquished by St George – the dragon being a well-understood type of the devil, sin, and unbelief. Minstrels, with music, clerks in surplices, and chaplains of the guild in splendid copes, chanting the joyful *Salve festa dies,* accompanied the procession to the church, where mass was celebrated." (11)

FUNDING

The cult of St George had come to the front rank from the time of Edward III onward, and any date from the mid 14th century might be possible for the founding of the Guild at St George's, Southwark. Perhaps its origins were linked to the rebuilding of the church in the 1390s? However, we have no evidence. The earliest surviving reference to the Guild in this parish appears to be a document found among a bundle of Chancery papers, now in the National Archives, and dated to between 1459 and 1465. (12)

This is a plea made by four men, who describe themselves as Wardens of the Fraternity, and it relates to a problem about the revenues. They complain of two other men, Thomas Went and William Lyng who, it seems, hold 'londes and tenements' belonging to the Guild, and whose rents are intended to supply part of its income. It appears that the money has been withheld, and they are making a legal plea to remedy the situation.

This does suggest that the Guild had been in existence for some time before that date – long enough not only to have acquired a portfolio of properties, donated by well-wishers to help provide an ongoing revenue, but also long enough for abuses to arise in connection with these.

Fund-raising tends to be a major part of the concern of any charitable body, and is one of the activities most likely to leave its trace in surviving records. Later in the same century, the Guild at St George's set out to improve their finances in another way. A Letter of Indulgence was obtained from Rome itself, giving direct approval of their activities, and offering the firm promise of remission from many days in Purgatory as an incentive to any donors.

We know of this, because the parish had copies produced for distribution – making use of the new technology of the printing press, now beginning to be exploited as a means of effective publicity. They were printed in English, and their wide circulation is suggested by the fact that three known copies have survived, each from separate printings.

Two of these are with the collection of Chancery documents, now in the National Archives. (13) They are almost identical, but there are small differences between them - where some of the line-breaks fall, and one or two variant abbreviations. More obviously, the small picture of St George and the Dragon, occupying the top left hand corner, is quite different in the two versions. They are both dated to 1st December

1514, but appear to come from two separate editions, by the same printer.

The document addresses itself "Unto all manere & synguler crysten people beholdynge or herynge these present letters". There follows a list of those in whose names the document is issued:
"Will'm's Ostin, Oliverus Albanem', Jacobus Tusculanen', Marcus Venistrien', Julianus Sabinen', cardynall bysshopes" and "Stephanus Praxede, Joh'es tit. de S'cto Marcello, Petrus tit. de Sancto Nicholae inter Imagines & Jeronimus tit. de Sancto Balbino, by the mercy of God Cardynal preestes of the holy chirche of Rome."

J.S. Brewer, who reprints most of the text in his Rolls Series collection of ***Letters and Papers*** for the reign of Henry VIII, says that this list of Cardinals indicates a date of 1479 for the issuing of the original letters. (14) This puts it back into the time when a man listed as 'John Gylis', but who we now know to have been Giovanni Gigli, was Rector of the parish. Gigli came to England as a Papal Collector, raising revenues for the See of Rome, and would have been well versed in the use of indulgences as a means of encouraging donors. In 1481 and 1489 he employed William Caxton to print indulgences, which were being issued in support of a crusade.

He was also employed by the English crown on diplomatic work, especially in relation to the Holy See. On 17th April 1479 he was appointed as a member of a mission which was sent by King Edward IV, to Pope Sixtus IV, to discuss a peace treaty with the French king. This means that we can securely place the Rector of St George's on a visit to Rome in the year when the Letter of Indulgence is likely to have been signed by the Cardinals. (15)

[illegible]
saynt George the martyr in Southwerke protecter & defender of th
me of Englande any thynge or helpe with any parte of theyr goode
Reparacios or mayntenynge the seruyce of almyghty god done in
me place / as in gyuyng any boke / belle / or lyght / or any other churchly ornamētes they sha
of eche vs Cardinalles syngulerly aforesayd a. C. dayes of pardon. ¶ Also there is foūde
same parysshe church aforesayd .iii. chauntre preest perpetually to pray in the sayd churche
bretherne & systers of the same fraternite & for the soules of theym that be departed & for all
sten soules. And also .iiii. tymes by the yere Placebo & Dirige with .xiiii. preestes & clerkes
iii. solempne masses one of our Lady / another of saynt George / with a masse of Requiem.
¶ Moreouer our holy fathers Cardynalles of Rome aforesayd haue graunted the pard
foloweth to all theym that be bretherne and systers of the same fraternite at euery of these f
lowyng / that is to say the first sonday after the feest of saynt Johñ baptyst / on the whiche d
same church was halowed .xii. C. dayes of pardon. ¶ Also the feest of saynt Mychaell y a
gell .xii. C. dayes of pardon. ¶ Also the seconde sonday in Lent .xii. C. dayes of pdon. ¶
good frydaye / the whiche daye Christe suffered his passion .xii. C. dayes of pardon. ¶ a
tewesdaye in the whytsonweke .xii. C. dayes of pardon. ¶ And also at euery feest of our la
syngulerly by hymselfe from the first euensong to the seconde euensong inclusiuely .xii. C.
of pdon. ¶ Also my lord Cardinall & chaūceller of Englande hath gyuen a. C. dayes of pa
¶ The sūme of the pardon cometh to in the yere .xii. M. CCCC. & .xl. dayes of p
¶ The summe of the masses that is sayd & song within the same parysshe churche o
George is a. M. and .xliiii. ¶ God saue the kynge.

Overleaf: One of the three known printings of the Letter of Indulgence obtained by Giovanni Gigli in Rome, in 1579, and circulated in the early 1500s, during the incumbency of Peter Carmelianus.

The text goes on to promise "on the authority of the apostles Peter and Paul", to any who "devoutly give to the guild or fraternity of St George in Southwark any thing or help with any parte of their goods to the reparation or maintaining the service of almighty God done in the same place" that they shall have one hundred days of pardon. It then lists a number of feasts and holy days on which this will apply.

At the bottom of the sheet we read that "These letters have been duely examyned by the right worthypfull mayster doctour Collet deane of Poules
mayster doctour Younge mayster of saynt Thomas of Acres
and mayster doctoure Horsey Chaunceler to the reverent fader
in god the bysshop of London."
This august group of clergymen apparently had the job of verifying that the letter was genuine, and that it could properly be used for the purpose of soliciting donations.

Finally, we are told that it was "Emprynted the yere of our Lord M.CCCCC. and xiiii. the fyrste daye of December." This is some 35 years after the Indulgence was first issued in Rome. Presumably the Fraternity began to make use of the letter to promote its fund-raising as soon as it was available to them. Perhaps their earlier use of it was more local, or more targeted. In 1502 a donation was made to the Guild by the Queen, Elizabeth of York. After this, there is record of donations being given by the King in most years. The royal donation was usually of one mark – 13s 4d.

In 1511 a grant of protection was made by the King, "for one year to the deputies of the Guild of the Virgin Mary and St George, in the church of St George, Southwark, sent to various parts of the country to solicit and collect alms." (16) This is the first evidence of the Fraternity casting its net beyond London, and was probably linked to the project of having printed copies of the letter of indulgence produced, for wider circulation.

Most of these surviving records of donations and active fund-raising are from the time when Peter Carmelianus was Rector. It looks very much as if he may have been using his connections at court to help promote the parish Fraternity and its good works. All of the printed copies of the letters that survive are also from his time. We know that Carmelianus had worked with some of the English printers from an early stage, and it may have been through his initiative and connections that the Guild came to seek wider publicity, exploiting the opportunities now being opened up by this new medium.

The third surviving copy of the letter, now in the possession of the Society of Antiquaries, is dated to 1518. (17) It is said to have been produced by the royal printer Richard Pynson. Carmelianus would appear to have had an association with Pynson stretching over more than a decade. He contributed verses to a publication by Pynson describing ***The Solempnities and triumphes doon and made at the spousells and Mariage of the Kings daughter the Lady Marye to the Prince of Castile Archduke of Austrige*** in 1508. After the Battle of Flodden, an epitaph on the defeated King James IV of Scotland, by Carmelianus, was included with a tract issued by the printer, probably in 1513. Again, around 1520, when Pynson published a poem on the 'Four Virtues' by Dominici Mancini, Carmelianus wrote a six line verse to add to the publication. (18)

This third and latest version of the Letter shows a number of variations from the two earlier editions. Saint George is described as 'protector and defender of this realme of Englande' and then more detail is given of the sort of gifts people might be encouraged to give: "...any thynge or helpe with any parte of thyr goodes to the Reparaciõs or maynteynyge the service of Almighty God done in the same place as in gyvynge any boke or belle or lyght or any other churchly ornamе[n]tes..." This version also tells us that "...there is fou[n]ded in the same parysshe church aforesayd iii chantre preests p[er]petually to pray in the sayd Churche for the brethren and systers of the same fraternite and for the souls of theym that be departed and for all chrysten soules."

A PLACE OF PILGRIMAGE?

If someone, receiving a copy of one of the Letters of Indulgence, was moved to make a gift to St George's, how would they have got it there? They couldn't just put a cheque in the post. There were carriers but, with something valuable, especially with a gift that had religious meaning, there was no substitute for taking it in person.

To make a special journey to the church, in order to leave your gift and receive remission from time in Purgatory, would give the venture something of the character of a pilgrimage. St George's stood close to the starting point of one of the main pilgrim routes to Canterbury, but could it really have attracted pilgrims in its own right? There is at least one piece of evidence that suggests that it did.

Later in the reign of Henry VIII the playwright, John Heywood, wrote ***The Play of the Foure P.P.*** The four Ps in question were the characters in the play – a Palmer, a Pardoner, a 'Potycary', and a Pedlar. The play opens with a speech by the Palmer – a kind of professional pilgrim - who reels off to the audience a list of all the shrines he has visited. He has been to Jerusalem, to Rome and to Compostela, but the majority of places on his list are English ones. He tells us he has been –

> At saynt Toncomber and saynt Tronion
> At saynt Botulph and saynt Anne of Buckston
> On the hylles of Armory where I see Noes ark
> With holy Job and saynt George in Suthwerke

The play is described as 'a newe and very mery enterlude' and the four characters dispute about who can do most good for people. When the Palmer comes to the end of his list of pilgrimages, the Pardoner tells him that whatever benefit had been gained from these journeys, he could have sold to him, without the need to leave home. There is probably deliberate humour here, in setting the exotic journey to Armenia to see Noah's Ark alongside the trip to St George's, a few hundred yards from London Bridge. (19)

Nevertheless, the fact that it is in the list at all is significant. Heywood may have been provoking laughter by counterpointing some of the premier destinations with local places that were barely in the lowliest league of shrines, yet the inclusion of St George's does suggest that some people considered it worth a journey. Most churches possessed a few relics, and it may well be that some alleged remains of St George himself had been acquired for the parish.

The principle place of pilgrimage to St George in England would have been the royal chapel at Windsor – where they had the skull, heart and several bones of the saint. Even so, a place to reverence the national saint in London itself, standing on a well-worn pilgrim route, could have had a certain attraction. Sending out the Letters of Indulgence may have been part of a more concerted attempt to promote the church as a place to visit, bringing gifts, and maybe looking for some small miracle.

Heywood was an accomplished musician, as well as writer, and was well thought of by Henry VIII. He was at court by 1519. He was also friendly with Thomas More, who acted as a patron to him, and introduced him to others in his circle. Through these connections he is likely to have known Peter Carmelianus, Rector of St George. Although a generation older, Carmelianus was still seen at court during that period. He was also well known to More, so there may be good reason why the writer, seeking an apt rhyme for ***Noah's Ark***, should have chosen a place as local as ***St George in Southwark***.

THE END OF THE GUILDS

This period, when the Fraternity was able to sustain three priests may well have been its most flourishing time. Within a generation, everything was changed. By the 1530s the well-connected Rector, Carmelianus, had died and been replaced. After Henry VIII's break with the Pope, the restructuring of the English Church began, with the king's ministers on the lookout for revenues which could be appropriated to the Crown. After the monasteries had been dissolved, other religious societies, including Parish Guilds, began to look like possible targets.

In 1528 a pamphlet appeared, with the title ***Supplication of the Beggars***. It sought to petition the king on behalf of poor people, lepers, the lame and others, who were alleged to be losing out on alms, because the money was going to pay monks, friars and priests to say mass for souls in Purgatory. Why, it asked, does the Pope not deliver all souls from Purgatory, if he has the power to do so? Although no less a person than Thomas More was commissioned to write a rebuttal of the arguments, the controversy continued. Reforming ideas must have challenged the Guilds. It may well be that, even before there was a formal move against them, many were feeling it prudent not to look to be too well-endowed. (20) Certainly, by 1541, only one priest is being maintained by the Guild at St George's.

It was little more than a year before the death of Henry VIII that an Act was passed authorising the appropriation of property belonging to chantries, guilds, fraternities, chapels, colleges and hospitals, on the grounds that the resources were needed to finance the wars against France and Scotland. A survey was begun, but little action seems to have been taken before the king died. However, the reprieve was short-lived.

In the first year of Edward VI's reign a new Act was passed and commissioners appointed. Archbishop Cranmer and other bishops tried hard to delay the legislation, and to protect the educational and charitable work of the guilds. Some concessions were made, on paper at least, but most trace of the parish guilds and their work disappeared within the next year or two. The chaplains were pensioned off, on similar terms to those that had previously been offered to monks when the monasteries were closed.

The last records of the Guild at St George's are to be found among the papers of the commissioners. In the return of William Goodwynne the ***Fraternytie of Seynt George in the parisshe in Southwerke*** is listed, and the name of the 'Incumbent having stipend and other relief by the same' is 'Richard Gooday, incumbent there.' In the next column – 'The sums which the said persons had for their support or other relief by the foresaid Chantrys and Freechappels towards the payment of their tenths to the Kings majesty' – it gives the figure of £6. 2s. 8d., the tithe being 12s and 108s remaining as pension. (20)

There is also a 'Certificate of Robert Southwell, Thomas Pope, William Goringe, and others, as part of their survey in the county of Surrey, dated 14th February in the second year of Edward's reign (1548).

Southewarke
The broderhed of Our Lady and Seynte George founded for
the mayntenaunce of one pryeste for ever in the parysshe
churche of Seynte Georges in Southwerke to pray for Sowles
wythin whiche parysshe are Dccccxxj (921) houslinge people
and the same broderhed nowe being voyde of any incumbent
is valewed to be worth
in landes and tenementes by yere vj*li*. xj*s*. vii*d*. (£6. 11s. 7d)
whereof in rent
resolute ix*s*.(9s) and so remayneth clere vj*li*. ij*s*. viii*d*. (£6. 2s. 8d) (21)

So the medieval Guild of Our Lady and St George in Southwark passed out of existence, along with similar associations across the country. The pattern of parish life was to be reshaped during the Tudor period, with new responsibilities given to churchwardens and other officers. For the next century or two there was often a Protestant earnestness about local church affairs. The plays and other entertainments moved out into secular society. No one was urged to donate 'lights and churchly ornaments' because none were now used in the churches.

Church life and local society reshaped themselves; charitable giving found new outlets. By the nineteenth century parish activities were more varied and energetic than, perhaps, they had ever been. What came to an end was certain sense of the unity of local life, with the local church at its centre. Society was becoming more complex, skills and interests more specialised, as it moved from the medieval to the early modern world.

NOTES

1. Revd. W.J. Somerville, Annual Report delivered in 1902. Copy in Southwark Local Studies Library.
2. See J.G. Davies, "The Secular Use of Church Buildings" SCM Press 1968
3. Ida Darlington, "The Reformation in Southwark". Proceedings of the Hugenot Society of London, Vol. XIX, No. 3. 1955.
4. W. Rendle, "Old Southwark and Its People", p.73
5. See H.F. Westlake, *The Parish Guilds of Medieval England,* SPCK 1919 for a detailed study of these records.
6. *Parish Fraternity Register: Fraternity of the Holy Trinity and SS. Fabian and Sebastian in the Parish of St Botolph without Aldersgate.* Ed. and introduction by Patricia Basing. London Record Society 1982. p.vii.
7. ibid. p.viii.
8. ibid. p.xii.
9. Prologue, lines 507-10. St Paul's was where a clergyman would go, if looking for someone to take him on as a chaplain.
10. H.F. Westlake. ibid. p.45

11. From a newspaper article, almost certainly 'South London Press', in Southwark Local Studies Library. Close reading of the passage, with the repeated 'probably' indicates that Rendle was embroidering on information available from elsewhere, rather than drawing on any direct account of local proceedings.

12. PRO C1/28/203. The dating is from Martha Carlin.

13. PRO C270/35/12 & 13.

14. Brewer, *Letters & Papers of Henry VIII*, Vol 1, 1510, no. 221

15. B.R.U.O.

16. Brewer, *Letters & Papers of Henry VIII*, Vol 1, no. 833

17. Society of Antiquaries, Lemon 2.

18. See David Carlson, *The Occasional Poetry of Pietro Carmeliano.*

19. *The Dramatic Writings of John Heywood*, ed. John S. Farmer, 1905, Early English Drama Society

18. H.F. Westlake. ibid. p.128ff.

20. Theodore Craib, *"Surrey Chantries"*. Surrey Archaeological Collections 25. 1912, p.16, VIII

21 ibid. X. *L.R. Misc. Bks 215*

480
BREVIARY OF
TÉROUANE.
BRIT. MUS.
ADDITIONAL
36,672.
d5

Overleaf: The outer binding of the Breviary of Terouanne

(B.L. Addit. 36672)

STOLEN GOODS?
THE BREVIARY OF TEROUANNE

The printed Letters of Indulgence distributed in 1514, encouraging people to make donations in support of the Parish Guild of St George's, promised remission of days in Purgatory, not only for those making cash donations, but also encouraged people to "helpe with any parte of theyr goodes to the Reparaciõs or maynteynyge the service of Almighty God done in the same place as in gyvynge any boke or belle or lyght or any other churchly ornamëtes". We know that some people did make such gifts in kind. In particular, we know of one book which was given to the church during this period, and which was of exceptional quality, though also of rather dubious provenance.

This book in question, known as *The Breviary of Therouanne*, is now in the possession of British Library, and bears the catalogue mark: BL Add. 36672.

It was made in the 14th Century, for the Church of Therouanne, in northern France. The binding is old, and of wooden boards, covered with skin, with brass studs in the front and back. It has, however, been rebound at some point, as three paper pages have been added to the front and back.

The book itself is written in Gothic text on vellum. It has 270 leaves.

A Breviary is a prayer book, and the contents consist of a Calendar, the Psalter, Propers and Gospels for Sundays and for Saints Days, Offices for the Blessed Virgin Mary and for the Dead, Benedictions and Order for the Common of Saints.

There are blue and gold initials on many of the pages, and a small number of larger decorated initials. In the second half of the book these large initials cease, but the scribe begins to extend some of the capital letters up to the top margin, with decorative flourishes. The impression given is of someone trying to maintain their interest in a lengthy task.

On the back of folio 68 is an account of how the book came into the possession of St George the Martyr, Southwark. This page has been written in the rather erratic script of someone who was almost certainly not a practised scribe. The British Library Catalogue transcribes the passage as follows:

"Thys boke I James Lyncolin I beqweyett hefter my desses to the chyrche off Sainte Gorge in Sotwarke att London wethowte hony excep off my yeff or off hony man hels. For this boke com from Hedyng in Fraince the XIII were off the ryng of kyng Hary the VIII and yet was take the XXIIIIth day off September and the yere of yowre lord Goode a M.CCCC and II and XXti and the was att takyng wet me of this boke a wong man that was calde John Tyeffyn and welde the same tyme in Sotwarke for yet was take from a france man be syde Hedyng VIII myle the XXIIII day off September."

Rendered into modern English, it could read:

"This book, I James Lincoln, bequeath after my decease to the church of Saint George in Southwark in London, without any exception of my wife or of any other man. For this book came from Hedyng in France, in the 13th year of the reign of king Henry VIII, and it was taken on the 23rd day of September in the year of our Lord God 1522, and there was with me at the taking of this book a young man that was called John Tiffen, who dwelled at the same time in Southwark, for it was taken from a Frenchman 8 miles outside Hedyng, the 24th day of September."

`Hedyng' is identified as the town of Hesdin, which is about 30 miles from Therouanne. At the time in question, England and France were officially at war, and a sporadic campaign of low level raids and skirmishes was being carried on. In September 1522 Hesdin was besieged by an English force, led by the Earl of Surrey. The siege failed, for lack of adequate artillery, but the army is said to have returned to Calais in October, with a good deal of plunder.

Surrey's campaign was something of a free-lance affair, and plunder may have been one of its main aims. It is tempting to see these two young men from Southwark, enlisting with the Earl for a bit of adventure and whatever they could get out it. It rather sounds as if, during the boring period of the siege, they wandered off and mugged a French civilian, possibly a monk or a priest, who had in his possession this valuable book. Was this a kind of sixteenth century version of football hooliganism?

However their prize had been acquired, they brought the book back home. Now, possibly feeling a few pangs of conscience, it is decided to unload their booty by donating it to the local church, with the hope of gaining some remission of sins in the process. In fact, since most of the great families of England had increased their wealth with French plunder from the wars of the previous two centuries, such action would probably not have seemed at all reprehensible at the time. James Lincoln treated his prize as a kind of insurance, choosing to cash it in for spiritual benefits in the life to come, rather than material profit in the present world.

The book is not likely to have remained in the possession of St George's for very long. Little more than ten years afterward, King Henry's quarrel with Rome began. In the Reformation that followed, all Latin service books would be supplanted by the English Prayer Book, and churches were expected to dispose of them. The Breviary, which had come to St George's by rather dubious means, may well have left there illicitly as well. Someone decided that the book was too good to be destroyed and probably hid it away. In the later sixteenth century, when there were plots to replace Queen Elizabeth with a Catholic successor, the mere possession of such a volume could have invited dangerous suspicion.

So well hidden was it that nothing certain is known of the volume for the next three hundred years, not until the mid nineteenth century. When it came to light again, it was in the private possession of a clergyman at Gloucester. The British Museum acquired it in a sale at Sothebys in 1902.

REPAIR AND REBUILDING

Scarcely anything can be said about the size, style or appearance of the original church on the site, other than that it was dedicated to St George. The report on the archaeological investigation carried out in conjunction with the recent restoration work states that 'No Saxo-Norman features, deposits or even residual pottery was found on the site'. This may have been due to its destruction by later grave digging or building works. Among the foundations, the earliest section of mortared ragstone and gravel wall foundation, 'which in stylistic grounds could be of 12th century date', is interpreted as possibly part of the south wall of the medieval nave (1)

The earliest documentary evidence for building works on the site is to be found in the Bridgemasters' Account Roll for 1391. In the Roll that runs from Michaelmas, in the 15th year of the reign of Richard II, there is a list of 'expenses on Saturday 4th November'. Along with the record of payments to chaplains, carpenters, masons, daubers, and for hurdles and paving, there is an item that reads:

Also paid for rebuilding of the church of St George's, Southwark, on behalf of lands belonging to London Bridge in the parish of the said church, and taxed for the aforesaid rebuilding, 10s. (2)

It looks as though the cost of building works on the church was raised – or at least part of it – by levying a rate on properties within the parish. The Bridgemasters owned land within St George's parish, and were taxed accordingly. (3) Whether 1391 was the actual year in which the works were carried out is not possible to say, but we may presume that they date from some time close to that year.

This 'rebuilding' has often been interpreted as meaning a total reconstruction, as radical as the one that was carried out in the

1730s. However, it might equally well imply major works – repairing walls, replacing the roof, maybe extending the building – a renewal of the structure, that maybe altered its outward appearance, whilst still retaining the basic shape and orientation. Certainly the archaeology appears not to distinguish two distinct medieval churches, but rather to suggest a series of additions and alterations, with various fragments of foundation and masonry dating 'from c.1200-1600'. The impression seems to be more of a progressive expansion – extending eastward, adding northern and southern transepts – but all developing on an original footprint.

Those first documented works date to about 290 years from the foundation, though doubtless there would have been other repairs needed before that time. Whilst a further three centuries were to elapse before the total rebuilding, evidence is beginning to be assembled, showing another phase of major building works in the early 16th century.

The recent excavations brought to light a series of pier bases, running along the presumed line of the north wall of the medieval nave. The building materials confirmed them as being later than the mid 15th century. In their foundations 'an estimated 190 fragments of reused Tudor architectural terracotta' were found. (4) Terracottas of this type are distinctive and dateable to the early Tudor period. Brandon Place, built by the Duke of Suffolk in the late 1520s, facing St George's on the other side of Borough High Street, is considered to be one of 'five key sites for the early use of terracotta in the English Renaissance during the 1520s.' (5) Surviving examples from Brandon place are held by the Cumin Museum.

Brandon Place was short-lived. (6). Charles Brandon, Duke of Suffolk, sold it to the king, in exchange for another property. Queen Mary gave it to the Archbishop of York, who then sold it on. The new purchasers seem to have been property developers, who demolished the building in the late 1550s and the site was turned to high-density residential use. Building materials are known to have been sold from the site, and it is suggested that this may date the construction work at St George's to around 1560. However, there is no documentary evidence and it could also be possible that the terracottas were acquired at the time of the construction of Brandon Place – either as breakages or surplus stock – thirty years earlier.

We know that there was active fund-raising for the parish, during the early Tudor period. The Letter of Indulgence, obtained in Rome by Giovanni Gigli in 1479 and re-printed several times during the years when Peter Carmelianus was Rector, was a main instrument for this. (7). The terms of the Indulgence suggest that it was initially directed toward support for the on-going worship and other activities of the Guild. However, the tempo of the fund-raising does seem to have increased in the early 1500s, with a grant of royal protection in 1511 for deputies of the Guild to be 'sent to various parts of the country to solicit and collect alms'. (8) This could perhaps be because some larger building scheme was now being planned.

One focus of current research is on the wills of parishioners during this period, some of which allude to building works under way. One bequest of 1515 seems to be tied to plans for some future 'takying down of the church and towards the buyldyng of the said church'. However, any such plans must have taken time to achieve, as a will of 1527 leaves money to St George's on condition that 'they procede in fynnysshing of the same newe worke fectually' (9) Most of the other relevant wills seem to date from the 1530s onward and, whilst there are some mentions of the building works, the emphasis shifts towards people wanting to be buried in 'the new work of the church'.

There is further study to be done on this material, but the impression is of a building programme set in motion during the second half of Carmelianus' incumbency, and getting under way during his last decade, though not finished until after his death. As to what the work might have been, this remains unclear. There has been some attempt to argue that there was something like a total rebuilding. Another possibility would be the construction of the large north aisle which is known to have been added at some stage. This would have involved taking down the entire north wall of the church, and there may also have been a re-construction of the tower at the same time.

We only begin to get descriptions of the medieval church from the later part of its life, into the 17th century. By this time, the interior would have been radically altered as a consequence of the changes brought in with the Reformation. One of the fullest accounts of the building is given by an anonymous antiquarian, who visited a number of the local churches in the early 18th century. It is a hand-written description surviving as part of a work titled *Promiscuous Collections of Surry*, now in the British Library. (10) The writer tells us that –

"It is an old building the Pillars Arches and Windows being of the Modern Gothick Order 'tis pleasant enough and pretty spacious as being (beside that space included in the Rails of the Com[munion] Table) 69 foot in length and 60 in breadth in height about 35 foot tho the altitude of the steeple (which consists of a Tower and Turret and in it 8 tunable Bells) is about 98 foot."

The exterior of the building does appear in a number of drawings, notably in Wyngaerde's panorama, and also in Hogarth's *Southwark Fair*, though the latter was drawn just before it was pulled down and replaced with the present building.

The later descriptions of the interior are of its post-Reformation ordering, and give us little clue as to how it originally looked. The architecture was then described as 'modern Gothick' and mention is also made of the 'Tuscan' altarpiece. However, the medieval furnishing and decoration would have been swept away long since. The rood screen, statues of the saints, and any pictures on the walls would have been removed or painted over.

The bulk of the description consists of lists of memorial inscriptions, gravestones, and windows painted with coats of arms and texts recalling benefactors or church repairs. Most of these date from the 17th century, and give some picture of the life of parish then, especially of its more well-to-do inhabitants.

What is of interest for both the medieval and modern history of the building is what we can learn about the condition of the fabric in earlier times. The same writer, quoted above, remarks that "The floor...which now is very uneven would wonderfully ornam[en]t the Church if mended."

He also tells us that, "In the Glass of one of the windows in the North side of the Church are the following words very legible and well done
This Church Steeple and Gallery were repaired and new pew'd and beautified and the South Ile enlarg'd by the Parishioners with the assistance of these and other good Benefactors in the year of our Lord God 1629....and having by Gods Providence and its remoteness stood clear of the Fire an[n]o 1666 (I perceive by another inscription in gold letters on the key piece of the West inner door case that) it was beautified and repaired an[n]o 1682 and the Steeple again an[n]o 1705."

In the late 20th century, when the structure of St George's once again gave serious cause for concern, the question was raised as to whether the same causes had given rise to problems with the building right from the earliest times? From the available information, the following list of major works can be compiled:

1100/20 ***First church constructed***
1391/2 **'Rebuilding'**
c. 1520-4 **Major works** – at least partial rebuilding.

1606 A brief granted for **repairs**, when £114.9s.9d was collected.

1629 **Steeple and gallery repaired**, new pews and South aisle enlarged

1652 **Repairs to building and windows**

1682 **Repaired** and beautified

1702 Contract for new organ

1705 **Repairs to Steeple**

1715/16 New pews and beautified

1733/6 ***Total reconstruction - medieval church replaced by current building***

1742 Galleries lowered, pews added and church beautified

1781 **Repaired** and beautified

1791 **Steps repaired** and altered

1806/8 **Substantial repair costing £9000.** Church closed for a year. Interior remodelled

1857 East window

1897 New ceiling

1899 Crypt cleared of bodies

1930 **Repairs to tower, spire and crypt – insufficient funds to complete**

1938 **Work on South wall and foundations, also roof beams**

1951/2 **Post-War restoration**

2004/8 **New foundations & roof; creation of new crypt.**

This is by no means a comprehensive list, especially for the earlier period, and all large buildings require periodic repair and maintenance. Nevertheless, there do seem to have been recurrent issues with the tower and the walls and, taken together with the rebuilding, could suggest that there are underlying problems which have persisted ever since the original foundation. The comment on the condition of the floor, in the early 1700s, could be added to this list. Much the same could well have been said of the floor of St George's by the 1990s, when the flagstones had become uneven, the aisles sloped, and the doors kept on binding, however often they were eased.

Extensive investigations carried out in 1997 led the Consulting Engineers to conclude "that the structure appears to be generally founded on made ground overlying a thin layer of clay.....The movements noted with the structure are considered to be the result of differential settlements within the structure due to the inadequate founding strata." (11). Archaeology on various neighbouring sites was by then building up an increasingly clear picture of the early topography. There was some consensus, by the 1990s, that St George's was built over the site of a prehistoric stream bed, and that this could go a long way toward explaining the recurring structural problems.

More recent studies, however, have seen this view modified, suggesting rather that the building was set on the edge of a prehistoric stream-bed, that flowed along the south side of the site. The investigations carried out during work on the site itself revealed that it 'was not situated in the middle of palaeochannel, but instead it was located on an area of relatively high ground on the northern edge of a channel, which extended further south.' (12) There is some possible indication of more problems with the south wall than the north, over the centuries. Not only does there appear to have been less extensive building on the south side of the church than on the north, but one section of foundations discovered has been interpreted as that of a medieval chapel which was then taken down at an early period. (13) It is interesting that Wyngaerde's drawing appears to show no chapel or transept remaining on the south side of St George's – though this could be an artistic simplification.

Different ages will each have adopted their own strategies for dealing with structural problems. The most recent approach has been to try and resolve the underlying problems by creating an entire new foundation for the nave of church. At the same time the roof was renewed and repairs to the spire were carried out. As under-pinning involved the demolition of the existing crypt, the opportunity was taken to replace it with a much larger space, offering exciting new possibilities of use. The works were principally directed toward the conservation of a landmark building. St George's no longer had the 14th century privilege of being able to raise a tax on the properties in the parish, nor the Letters of Indulgence used in the 16th. However, the parish was able to draw on the valuable input of English Heritage, and the major assistance of the Heritage Lottery Fund, to see these works successfully carried through.

NOTES

1. MoLAS 2007, op.cit., p.18
2. Bridgemasters Account Roll, Roll 11, m.6. Corporation of London Record Office. MS translation by T.A.M. Bishop 1935.
3. It may be recalled that 'land of London bridge returning five *solidos* a year' was mentioned as part of the Ardern family's donation to Bermondsey Priory in 1122.
4. MoLAS 2007, op.cit. p.21
5. ibid. p.22
6. The extravagant exterior of the house is known mainly from Wyngaerde's panorama, drawn in the 1540s. See the first illustration in the book
7. See the chapter on the Guild for more detail on the Indulgence
8. PRO C270/35/12&13
9. Quoted from a paper by Dr Claire Martin, December 2008
10. BL Addit. MS 6409. fol 17ff.
11. Report by Hockley & Dawson, December 1997, 6.01 & 6.03.
12. MoLAS 2007, p.88
13. ibid. p.19.

www.ingramcontent.com/pod-product-compliance
Ingram Content Group UK Ltd.
Pitfield, Milton Keynes, MK11 3LW, UK
UKHW041435180426
11947UKWH00007B/463

9 780956 152114